GRDBK3717
Written by Rupert Frost
Images courtesy of PA Photos, Getty Images, Corbis Images
First published in 2012 by Go Entertainment Group Ltd.
© Go Entertainment Group Ltd 2012. All rights reserved.
Design ©2012 Go Entertainment Group Ltd.
This edition published by Go Entertainment Group Ltd
Broadley House, 48 Broadley Terrace,
London, NW1 6LG,
United Kingdom

Printed and bound in China

CONTENTS

> His most successful studio albums demonstrate a gift for finding dignity in the hardships of everyday American life.

INTRODUCTION

SINGER/SONGWRITER/PERFORMER
Bruce Springsteen is as American as John Wayne, Clint Eastwood and Cadillac cars. At 62, this musical star who has been a recording artist for 40 years shows no signs of burning out. 2012 sees the release of Springsteen's 17th studio album, *Wrecking Ball*, along with an accompanying world tour which began in March in Atlanta.

Blessed with monumental talent as a wordsmith and musician, Springsteen has maintained his position at the top of the rock world with a combination of diversity and integrity. Neither preacher nor pretender, he often wears his heart on his sleeve in a variety of musical genres but paints a believable canvas for listeners to interpret on their own

level. Promoted at the outset by his record company as a man who had "…more words in some individual songs than other artists had in whole albums", Springsteen also seems to have a greater collection of songs than many other artists put together. His recordings range from blockbusting rock albums to far more lugubrious folk-inspired creations, while his artistic calling card is American-focused 'heartland rock' interwoven with poetic, intense lyrics. Indeed, much of Springsteen's early output makes reference to the New Jersey shore where he spent his youth, and his most successful studio albums, *Born to Run* (1975) and *Born in the U.S.A.* (1984), demonstrate a gift for finding dignity in the hardships of

everyday American life. This marriage of autobiographical revelation and pumping beat has produced sales of more than 65 million albums in the U.S. for Springsteen, and more than 120 million worldwide. His work has received critical approval as well, earning him a variety of accolades including 21 Grammys, two Golden Globes and an Academy Award. Widely recognised as one of the most influential songwriters of the 20th century, Springsteen was voted the 23rd greatest rock 'n' roll artist of all time by *Rolling Stone* magazine in 2004, while American cable TV network VH1 has ranked him at No. 27 among its 100 Greatest Artists of Rock 'n' Roll and at No. 59 in its list of the 100 Sexiest Artists.

The young Springsteen, pictured in 1970s New Jersey.

The *Born To Run* era, 1975.

Since the breakthrough achieved by his third album, *Born to Run*, in 1975, Springsteen has remained a rare jewel among popular musicians: an artist who stays at the forefront of the recording and performing worlds, shifting millions of albums and selling out arenas round the globe year after year, as well as retaining widespread critical appreciation with gushing reviews reserved for his concerts and records. And although there have been a few hiccups along the way in Springsteen's career, the wonder of his nearly unbroken run of critical and commercial triumph is that he has attained it while occasionally challenging the listener with unexpected mutations in his style; he has followed his muse, even if that has changed his musical sound or the composition of his backup band, or made his lyrical message overtly political. Arguably, it may just be that these deviations have kept his image and music fresh, especially since Springsteen has always had the fallback of returning to what his fans think he does best: barnstorming the world with a marathon rock 'n' roll show that uses his reliable team The E Street Band.

He has followed his muse, even if that has changed his musical sound.

Bob Dylan, on tour in Stockholm, 1966.

As regards his musical influences and influence on his peers, Springsteen was inspired principally by Elvis, and he also shows a healthy respect for fellow American Bob Dylan. He has enthused artists that range from Tom Petty to U2 and The Killers, whose second album *Sam's Town* (2006) was motivated to some degree by his sound. The silver screen, too, has helped to mould Springsteen's identity. Many of his songs are visual landscapes, odd places infested with dangerous people – film noir worlds where the beauty of woman masks the beast within and betrayal awaits in the inky shadows.

Thematically, Springsteen's lyrical portfolio is as diverse as his variety of musical styles. Recurring threads in the narrative include the futility of war, the lurking spectre of violence and the vicissitudes of working-class life in America.

On stage with The E Street Band, 1975

But of all these subjects, the need to escape and the longing for elsewhere are the dominant forces, particularly in Springsteen's early days. The perfect example of the latter roared into eternity on the singer's most iconic song, *Born to Run*, where his feelings of worthlessness in the New Jersey environment delivered him to the freedom of the open road. Forget *Easy Rider* (1969), there was a new kid in town in the 70s, desperate to break out from the toil on society's fringes and taste the glamorous beyond:

The 'American dream' eluded him no longer.

Bruce wasn't the only one looking to escape New Jersey in the 1970s.

"In the day we sweat it out in the streets
Of a runaway American dream
At night we ride through mansions of
glory in suicide machines"

From the moment that the album *Born to*

Run launched Springsteen into the firmament of musical heroes, the 'American dream' eluded him no longer. All the 'mansions of glory' opened their doors to him as the record-buying public opened their wallets. But in a perfect twist of irony, Springsteen would abandon the ad-man's

fantasy of the Beverly Hills swank pad years later, and return to live in New Jersey: the place that had made him.

Two certainties emerge from this: Bruce Springsteen had captured the American dream and, in the process, had discovered his true home.

"Surprise surprise, come on open your eyes" – on stage in the 1970s.

GROWIN' UP

SITUATED ON THE Atlantic coast, the American state of New Jersey welcomed Bruce Frederick Joseph Springsteen into the world on September 23rd 1949. He was born in the city of Long Branch, part of Monmouth County, NJ, the eldest child of proud parents Douglas Frederick and Adele Ann Springsteen, who would provide Bruce with two younger sisters for company: Virginia, who was born in 1950, and a third arrival in 1962, Pamela, who would go on to enjoy minor success in slasher films towards the end of the 1980s before turning to

photography and shooting the covers for her brother's *Lucky Town* and *Human Touch* albums (1992).

Bruce grew up on South Street in Monmouth County's Freehold Borough, and was raised as a Roman Catholic. His father was of Irish/Dutch descent, employed principally as a bus driver, while his Italian mother – whose father had been born near Naples – worked as a legal secretary. The fiery character of the Italian South on his maternal side must have fuelled the passion for which Springsteen would become

known in his later life, but the boy's early education proved less than inspiring. He started out at the St. Rose of Lima Catholic School in Freehold Borough, where the sisters were far from merciful: "In the third grade a nun stuffed me in a garbage can under her desk because she said that's where I belonged." Rules and regulations seemed anathema to Springsteen at this stage, and he fared little better with the men of the cloth: "I also had the distinction of being the only altar boy knocked down by a priest during mass."

The streets of New Jersey, 1968.

The sight of Elvis Presley had already sown the seed of ambition in Springsteen.

The possibility of improved development in new surroundings came when Bruce moved on to the Freehold Borough High School in the ninth grade, but music was starting to dominate his thoughts even now. The sight of Elvis Presley gyrating on *The Ed Sullivan Show* in September 1956 had already sown the seed of ambition in Springsteen, who had determined to become a performer after witnessing the broadcast at the age of 7. His admiration for Presley is well known, and endures to this day: "He was as big as the whole country itself, as big as the whole dream… There have been a lot of tough guys. There have been pretenders. And there have been contenders. But there is only one King… Nothing will ever take the place of that guy."

Motivated by The King of Rock 'n' Roll to get his first guitar for the princely sum of 18 dollars at the age of 13, Springsteen came across as a withdrawn figure at high school, where he enjoyed his own company and adored his instrument of choice. Life back at home on South Street conformed to the same pattern: "When I was growing up, there were two things that were unpopular in my house. One was me, and the other was my guitar." But the teenage Bruce was at least encouraged by his mother, who took out a loan to buy her son a 60-dollar Kent guitar when he was 16. Who can imagine what would have happened to the future superstar without this maternal assistance? Bruce even toyed with the idea of being a baseball player before he concentrated fully on music! Study was certainly not his vocation, and he failed to turn up for his graduation ceremony at the end of high school. Thereafter he spent a short time at Ocean County College before throwing in the towel.

The Palace Amusements building in Asbury Park, NJ. The building famously featured a neon sign that read 'Tunnel Of Love', possibly inspiring Bruce's album of the same name.

The historic Café Wha?, pictured in 1970.

Bruce revealed his dislike of authority by acting up at the induction and refusing to take the tests.

Unless they are driven to perform as solo artists, most aspiring musicians need a band to play with. Having taken to the guitar resolutely as a 13-year-old, Springsteen joined his first group, The Castiles, at the age of 16 in 1965. With the assistance of local couple Tex and Marion Vinyard, who sponsored up-and-coming bands in town, Springsteen started out on lead guitar with the group before graduating to lead singer. The Castiles recorded two original numbers at a public recording studio in New Jersey's Brick Township and performed their Beatles-inspired music at various locations, including a spot at Cafe Wha? in New York's Greenwich Village.

Even at this primary stage of his career, Springsteen was expressing a desire to get to the top in the music business, but it would not be with The Castiles. They disbanded in 1967 around the time that the singer finished

high school and started visiting clubs in Asbury Park, NJ. The prospect of joining the war in Vietnam also scuppered the aspirations of the eighteen-year-old, but Bruce revealed his dislike of authority by acting up at the induction and refusing to take the tests. He was considered not acceptable for military service.

With his musical ambition back on track at this juncture, Springsteen had a short stint with a power trio called Earth, who played hard rock similar to British band Cream in the New Jersey clubs. Previously nicknamed 'Doctor', it was during this time in the late 1960s that Springsteen became known by his now-familiar moniker of 'The Boss'. The name came into being because Springsteen shouldered the responsibility of collecting a band's pay at gigs, and distributing the proceeds to his fellow musicians.

With Steve Van Zandt in New York, 2007.

Springsteen sought to shape a
uniquely genuine musical and
lyrical style of his own.

Also in the hard-rock mould was his next group, Child (soon to resurface as Steel Mill after the addition of guitarist-cum-vocalist Robbin Thompson), which featured Danny Federici on keyboards, Vini 'Mad Dog' Lopez on drums and Steve Van Zandt on bass. Bolstered by the introduction of bassist Vinnie Roslin, Steel Mill and Springsteen then enjoyed a three-year union that lasted from 1969 to early 1971, a period when they played both the mid-Atlantic college circuit and California. Following a Steel Mill gig in the golden state at the end of 1969, the respected *San Francisco Examiner* music critic Philip Elwood gave Springsteen credibility in his glowing assessment of the band in January 1970: "I have never been so overwhelmed by totally unknown talent." The journalist went on to praise the "cohesive musicality" of Steel Mill – who had, by now, received a contract offer from a record label – and, in particular, singled out Springsteen as "a most impressive composer." During this time Springsteen also performed regularly at small venues in Virginia and Massachusetts, as well as playing closer to home in Asbury

Park and along the Jersey Shore, where he milked his extensive local appeal and quickly gathered a cult following.

When his formative time in Steel Mill came to a close after the break-up of the group in 1971, Springsteen appeared in various guises over the next two years, as he sought to shape a uniquely genuine musical and lyrical style of his own. He created a short-lived big band that lasted from early to mid-1971, the psychedelic-sounding Dr. Zoom & the Sonic Boom, which was followed in rapid succession by The Sundance Blues Band (mid-1971) and The Bruce Springsteen Band (from mid-1971 to mid-1972). The latter group included The Boss's trusty colleagues Danny Federici, Vini Lopez and Steve Van Zandt – who was now on guitar – while the addition of Garry Tallent on bass and David Sancious on piano formed the heart of what would become The E Street Band, Springsteen's future backing group (occasional extras included a horn section – replaced by a single saxophonist, Clarence Clemons – Dr. Zoom's female backing singers The Zoomettes and Southside Johnny Lyon on harmonica).

Southside Johnny Lyon in Asbury Park, 1976.

Musical styles explored by The Bruce Springsteen Band ranged from blues, church music, jazz and R&B to early rock 'n' roll and soul, but The Boss split up his collective due to a lack of engagements. Next, Springsteen began playing shows alone in New York City, where his prodigious ability as a songwriter and his solo performances attracted the attention of management duo Mike Appel and Jim Cretecos. The former set up an audition for his new discovery with legendary Columbia Records talent scout John Hammond, the man who had secured the label's signature of a certain Bob Dylan the previous decade. Adhering to his own mantra of "When it comes to luck, you make your own", Springsteen took his opportunity with both hands, auditioning for Hammond in May 1972 and signing to Columbia in June.

The Boss pictured in 1977.

Born To Run, 1975.

This gathering of his
New Jersey-based colleagues
marked the genesis of
The E Street Band.

THIRD TIME LUCKY

ENTHUSED BY THE prospect of cutting his first album, Springsteen showed his allegiance to many of his old band members by requisitioning Clemons, Federici, Lopez, Sancious and Tallent for the forthcoming sessions. Van Zandt received the call-up too, but would spend little time in New York's 914 Sound Studios owing to a tour commitment as part of The Dovells' backing group. Despite Van Zandt's (near) absence, this gathering by The Boss of his New Jersey-based colleagues marked the genesis of The E Street Band, although it would not be formally named as such for several more years. Springsteen was a man on a mission at this moment, finally aware of his purpose

and destiny: "Until I realised that rock music was my connection to the rest of the human race, I felt like I was dying, for some reason, and I didn't know why."

The singer's debut LP was entitled *Greetings from Asbury Park, N.J.*, with the recording sessions lasting from early July to early September 1972. At first, Columbia Records planned to release the disc at the end of November that year, but eventually unleashed it on the market on January 5th 1973.

Initial sales were slow, with only 25,000 copies shifted in the first year of its release, although the album would later achieve double-platinum status (2 million copies sold)

and be ranked No. 379 by *Rolling Stone* on its list of the 500 greatest all-time albums.

As for the singles' market, Columbia put out two tracks off *Greetings from Asbury Park, N.J.*, but neither *Spirit in the Night* nor *Blinded by the Light* – the album's opening song – made any waves in the U.S. charts. Ironically, Manfred Mann's Earth Band released a version of *Blinded by the Light* on their album *The Roaring Silence*, which reached No. 1 on Billboard's Hot 100 on 19th February 1977 and No. 1 on the Canadian RPM chart the same day. Although hard to believe, the latter recording of *Blinded by the Light* represents Springsteen's only No. 1 single as a songwriter on the Hot 100.

Chart positions and financial considerations aside, *Greetings from Asbury Park, N.J.* made more of an impact with the critics, even if the debutant Springsteen was the object of comparison rather than direct adulation.

Because of his lyrical poeticism and folk rock-rooted music exemplified on tracks like *Blinded by the Light* and *For You*, as well as the Columbia and Hammond connections, Bob Dylan became the obvious point of reference: "He sings with a freshness and urgency I haven't heard since I was rocked by *Like a Rolling Stone*" wrote *Crawdaddy* magazine editor Peter Knobler in Springsteen's first interview/profile in March 1973. And music journalist Lester Bangs wrote in *Creem* magazine in 1975 that when Springsteen's first album was released, "... many of us dismissed it: he wrote like Bob Dylan and Van Morrison, sang like Van Morrison and Robbie Robertson, and led a band that sounded like

Van Morrison's".

The track *Spirit in the Night* was influenced by Van Morrison for sure, but *Lost in the Flood* had the stamp of Springsteen in its depiction of Vietnam veterans, and *Growin' Up* marked a first stab by The Boss at his recurring theme of adolescence. He had a voice of his own, undoubtedly, and experience would take care of the fine-tuning.

As he developed his musical identity on the follow-up to *Greetings from Asbury Park, N.J.* in 1973, Springsteen suffered none of the problems that often befall an artist's second album. Nevertheless, *The Wild, the Innocent & the E Street Shuffle* was greeted with little fanfare commercially upon its September 11th release, despite receiving some rave reviews (the record has since achieved the double-platinum status of its predecessor and in 2003 was placed at No. 132 by *Rolling Stone* magazine in their list of the 500 greatest albums of all time).

BRUCE SF
INNOCE

On stage in the 1970s.

RINGSTEEN: THE WILD, THE
IT & THE E STREET SHUFFLE

He had a
voice of his own,
undoubtedly,
and experience
would take
care of the
fine-tuning.

"On a night when I needed to feel young, he made me feel like I was hearing music for the very first time"

Critics of the era warmed to the collaboration of Springsteen and his (still unnamed) E Street Band, whose output was noticeably grander in form and scope, with a less folky, more R&B vibe complementing lyrics that often romanticised the stresses of teenage life. *Incident on 57th Street* would become a fan favourite, while the rousing *Rosalita (Come Out Tonight)* continues to rank among the Springsteen faithful as one of their most beloved closing numbers at concerts.

The similarly adored *4th of July, Asbury Park (Sandy)* made direct reference to Springsteen's stamping ground in Monmouth County, and the album's obscure title was rooted in fact. The E Street Band took its name from an address in Belmar, New Jersey: the mother of pianist David Sancious lived at 1107 E Street and allowed the group to rehearse in her garage. As for the 'Shuffle', history would have it that the band's rented truck broke down late one night on their return home to New Jersey after a gig in New York City. Within walking distance of Sancious's mother's house, the group 'shuffled' their way back on foot to 1107 E

Street through the snow.

A year after the release of *The Wild, the Innocent & the E Street Shuffle*, Springsteen altered the line-up of his support – who were now named The E Street Band – and toured extensively to promote the album. Roy Bittan and Max Weinberg joined, replacing David Sancious and Vini Lopez on piano and drums respectively. During this period on the road in 1974, Springsteen caught the eye of music journalist Jon Landau with a spectacular concert in Massachusetts: "I saw rock 'n' roll's future, and its name is Bruce Springsteen. And on a night when I needed to feel young, he made me feel like I was hearing music for the very first time".

Thereafter, Landau became Springsteen's manager and producer, signalling the departure of the singer's first guru, Mike Appel. With the aid of his new mentor, Springsteen resolved to finish his epic third album, *Born to Run*, the LP that represented his final chance with Columbia Records.

"Blinded By The Light", 1978.

Given a huge budget in a last-ditch effort at a commercially viable product, Springsteen became bogged down in the recording process while striving for a multi-layered, wall-of-sound experience in the style of producer extraordinaire Phil Spector. The album's complicated arrangements took more than 14 months to record, during which time most of the tracks were laid down by a core rhythm section comprising Springsteen, Weinberg, Bittan and bassist Garry Tallent, while other musicians' contributions were then bolted on at a later stage. Six months alone were spent perfecting the song *Born to Run*, which Springsteen wanted to resemble "Roy Orbison singing Bob Dylan, produced by Spector."

Springsteen had a keen regard for Bob Dylan, appreciating the brain that kindled the inception of a quality sound: "Bob freed your mind the way Elvis freed your body. He showed us that just because music was innately physical did not mean that it was anti-intellectual. He had the vision and the talent to make a pop record that contained the whole world."

Springsteen's own talent and vision were unquestionable now, but his creative process on *Born to Run* was fraught with self-doubt. The singer battled with anger and frustration in the studio, claiming to hear sounds in his head that he could not explain to his fellow musicians, although trusty colleague Steve Van Zandt provided a calming influence for Springsteen by organising the horn section on *Tenth Avenue Freeze-Out* – his only written contribution to the album (Van Zandt would soon become a vital part of The E Street Band).

By the end of the mammoth recording sessions for *Born to Run*, Springsteen was still not satisfied. At the outset, he had intended to deliver a concept album, bookending the record with different versions of the track *Thunder Road*. But in terms of the finished LP's sequencing, he eventually produced a 4-cornered disc, since the songs that opened each side (*Thunder Road, Born to Run*) were uplifting odes to escape, while the songs that closed each side (*Backstreets, Jungleland*) were sorrowful epics of betrayal, defeat and loss.

The singer battled with anger and frustration, claiming to hear sounds in his head that he could not explain to his fellow musicians.

THE BOTTOM LINE, Cabaret

CURRENTLY APPEARING
PAUL BRADY

O RIK EMMETT
2 NASHVILLE'S BLUEB
4 AL STEWART
5 CASSANDRA REE
7 LINA KOUTRAK

THE BOTT

Artists are temperamental creatures at the best of times, and Springsteen's first reaction to the finished album was to throw it into the street! He told his manager Jon Landau that he would rather just cut the record live at New York's Bottom Line club, where he played regularly. But even if he had compromised his initial vision for *Born to Run*, Springsteen's response to his own material was ill judged. The songwriting and recording were more disciplined than before, while still maintaining

an epic feel. With its panoramic imagery, thundering production and desperate optimism, *Born to Run* is considered by some fans to be among the best rock 'n' roll albums of all time and Springsteen's magnum opus. In particular, the opening track *Thunder Road* marked a high point for the New Jersey singer/songwriter, and took its name from the eponymous movie starring Robert Mitchum.

Co-written, produced and based on an original story by the actor, the 1958 crime

drama revolved around the illegal production of whisky in rural America, and remains something of a cult curio. In Springsteen's hands, the exhilarating story evoked the thrill of love and adventure against a beckoning US backdrop:

"Well the night's bustin' open
These two lanes will take us anywhere
We got one last chance to make it real
To trade in these wings on some wheels"

New York's Bottom Line Club, 2003

Springsteen's first reaction to the finished album was to throw it into the street.

The 'Garden State' of New Jersey, seen here in 1968, has its share of highways.

He was no Dylan clone, but rather a unique talent cast in the furnace of blue-collar America.

Here, Springsteen's harmonica playing conjured images of the wandering troubadour, yet he was no Dylan clone, but rather a unique talent cast in the furnace of blue-collar America. As for the album's title track, the fusion of Springsteen's guitar and Ernest 'Boom' Carter's thumping drums gave full demonstration of the singer's trademark style. Backed up by the harmonious saxophone interlude from Clarence Clemons, *Born to Run* was the definitive showcase of Springsteen at his raw, energetic best. You could almost smell the exhaust on Highway 9 as The Boss's gravelly vocals raged on behalf of those who were trapped within the confines of small-town America. This was a voice burning with vitriol, soaked in the bitter honey of experience. Springsteen's view of the song was ambition personified: "My shot at the title. A 24-year-old kid aimin' at the greatest rock 'n' roll record ever."

Born to Run captured the heaviness of Springsteen's earlier releases while displaying a more diverse range of influences, and the buzz for the New Jersey boy was getting louder. On August 13th 1975, Springsteen and The E Street Band began a five-night, 10-show stint at The Bottom Line in New York. The engagement attracted major media attention, was broadcast live on the radio, and convinced many sceptics that Springsteen was for real. And, fed by the playing of an early mix of *Born to Run* on progressive rock radio, anticipation built to fever pitch before the album's release. With the arrival of *Born to Run* on August 25th 1975, Springsteen at last found critical and commercial success, as the breakthrough album cemented the reputation he had earned from the music press and his significant cult audience. Rather than representing an example of third time lucky for its creator, the album pointed more to obsessive dedication and immaculate musicianship.

On stage at the Bottom Line Club, 1975.

Even though it had no No. 1 singles, *Born to Run* helped Springsteen to reach mainstream popularity.

Peaking at number 3 on the Billboard 200, it became Springsteen's first gold disc in America (500,000 copies) and would eventually sell six million copies in the U.S. by the year 2000. Even though it had no No. 1 singles, *Born to Run* (Billboard No. 23) helped Springsteen to reach mainstream popularity – the Holy Grail for any savvy artist – while *Thunder Road*, *Tenth Avenue Freeze-Out* (Billboard No. 83) and *Jungleland* all received massive album-focused airplay. They remain firm favourites at concerts and on many classic rock stations, and the album is listed in the Library of Congress's National Recording Registry of historic recordings. Ranked at No. 18 by *Rolling Stone* on their list of The 500 Greatest Albums of All Time, *Born to Run* is widely considered Springsteen's masterpiece, the work that catapulted his career and transformed his identity from Jersey-bound act to acclaimed national and international artist.

It established him as a sincere, dynamic rock 'n' roll personality who spoke for and in the voice of a large contingent of the rock audience. His first two albums had received good reviews, but popular success had been scarce. Now, Springsteen had fully emerged as the toast of 1975. The media warmed to the singer and his brand, adding the icing to a very impressive cake. On October 27th, both *Time* and *Newsweek* splashed the face of the New Jersey boy all over their front covers – an honour usually reserved for heads of state (although some might still argue to this day that Mr Springsteen would make an inspirational leader). So great did the waves of publicity and spiralling hype become that Springsteen eventually rebelled against it during his first venture overseas, tearing down promotional posters before a concert appearance in London.

Live on stage, 1974.

He may have torn down posters for his first London shows, but his popularity there would only grow, as evidenced at this Wembley Stadium concert in 1985.

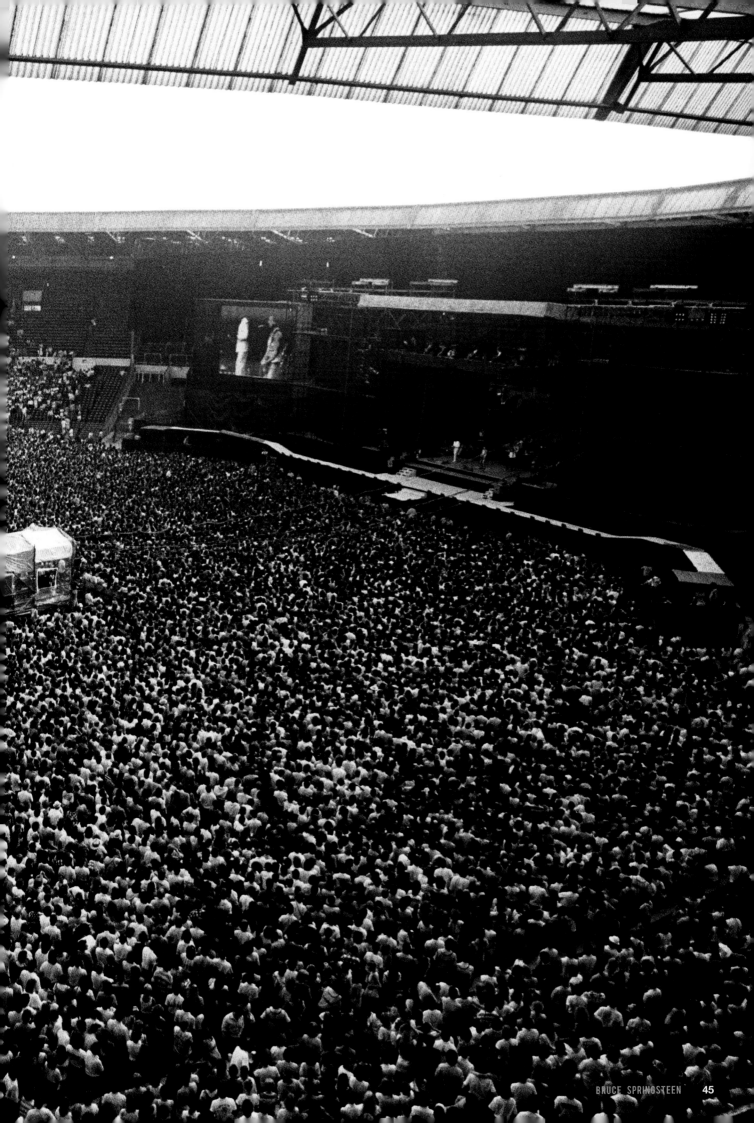

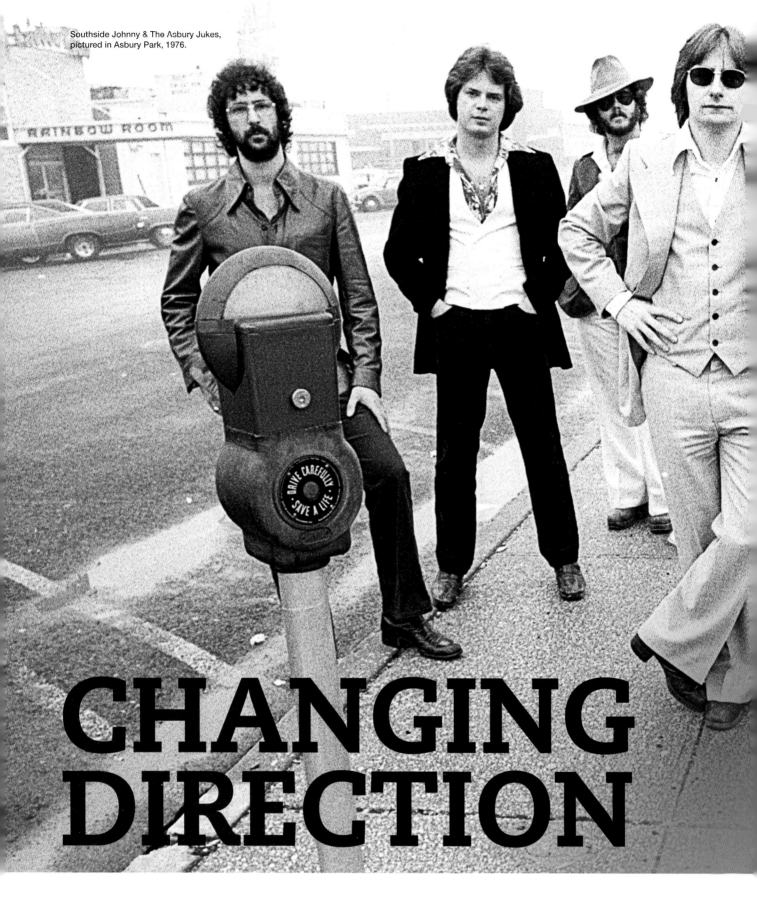

Southside Johnny & The Asbury Jukes, pictured in Asbury Park, 1976.

CHANGING DIRECTION

SPRINGSTEEN'S MOMENT OF triumph with *Born to Run* came to an abrupt halt after the record's release, as his new creative association with Jon Landau and resultant separation from former manager Mike Appel ended in legal proceedings. The singer's ensuing dispute with Appel was brought on by contractual obligations and only resolved in 1977 when the pair reached a settlement. In the interim, Springsteen could not record

in the studio, yet he remained active artistically and took The E Street Band on tour throughout the United States. He often played with optimistic fervour, but his latest songs had adopted a more sombre tone than much of his former material.

As he battled the stress of the legal wrangling and the expectation of further success after *Born to Run*'s breakthrough, Springsteen retreated to New Jersey during

> The songs seemed leaner and more carefully drawn, reflecting Springsteen's growing intellectual and political awareness.

the enforced period of hiatus. His agenda was clear: "More than rich, more than famous, more than happy, I wanted to be great." He finally started recording his fourth studio album in 1977, the result of which was released as *Darkness on the Edge of Town*. When it came out on June 2nd 1978, the somewhat less commercial disc evidenced a turning point in The Boss's musical career. Gone were the raw, rapid-fire lyrics, outsized characters and long, multi-part compositions of the previous albums. Now the songs seemed leaner and more carefully drawn, reflecting Springsteen's growing intellectual and political awareness. This record was far more low-key than its predecessors, and its moody material sounded more intimate.

In many respects, Springsteen had had to reinvent himself with *Darkness on the Edge of Town*. By now, record labels had signed their own brand of The Boss's 'heartland rock' sound, in such similar artists as Bob Seger & The Silver Bullet Band (who actually preceded Springsteen but achieved national recognition in his wake), Johnny Cougar (aka John Mellencamp), Tom Petty & The Heartbreakers, Meat Loaf, Eddie Money, and even fellow Jersey Shore residents Southside Johnny & the Asbury Jukes (pictured).

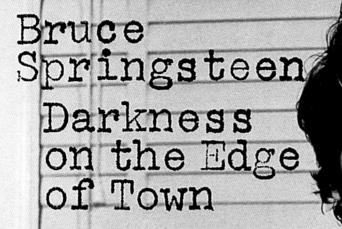

Bruce Springsteen Darkness on the Edge of Town

At the same time, the punk/new-wave explosion had become the new focus of critical devotion, making Springsteen seem unfashionable. Notwithstanding these challenges, *Darkness...* earned its share of good reviews as critics admired Springsteen's heartfelt ode to home and small-town hardship. While aspiring to greatness at the outset, the artist's extra intentions had also been clear: "This was the record… where I figured out what I wanted to write about, the people that mattered to me, and who I wanted to be. I saw friends and family struggling to lead decent, productive lives and I felt an everyday kind of heroism in this." These sentiments were echoed succinctly on the opening track *Badlands*, where drummer Max Weinberg and Springsteen's regular band members

provided solid accompaniment to the homespun wisdom:

"Badlands, you gotta live it every day
Let the broken hearts stand
As the price you've gotta pay"

Darkness... achieved Top Ten status, going platinum (1 million copies sold) within weeks of hitting the shops, before going on to sell 3 million. Despite producing no major hit singles, the presence of *Prove It All Night* at No. 33 on the U.S. Top 40 – and of its follow-up, *Badlands*, at 42 – ensured that Springsteen's fourth album remained on the charts for 97 weeks. A cross-country tour also ensued in 1978 to promote the record's release, and the intensity of the live Springsteen

experience was by now legendary. Away from the performing arena at this stage of the late 1970s, The Boss had also improved his profile in the pop world, earning a reputation as a songwriter whose material could provide hits for other artists: Manfred Mann's Earth Band had achieved a U.S. No. 1 pop hit with a heavily rearranged version of *Blinded by the Light* in early 1977; Elvis had been the inspiration behind the song *Fire* in the mid 1970s, which eventually saw the light of day in early 1979 when The Pointer Sisters took it to No. 2 in the Top Ten; and another recipient of Springsteen's creativity was Patti Smith, to whom he gave the composition *Because the Night*, which, with some lyrical tweaks by Smith, became her only Top 40 hit when it reached No. 13 in the spring of 1978.

Patti Smith, performing at a tribute concert to Bruce Springsteen, 2007.

The intensity of the live Springsteen experience was by now legendary.

A year later in September, Springsteen rounded off the decade that made a star out of him by joining with The E Street Band and the Musicians United for Safe Energy anti-nuclear power collective at Madison Square Garden for two nights, playing an abbreviated set while premiering two songs from his next work. The subsequent *No Nukes* live album, as well as the following summer's *No Nukes* documentary, represented the first official recordings and footage of Springsteen's fabled live act, as well as The Boss's first tentative dip into political involvement. There would be more to come...

Performing at the Musicians United For Safe Energy concert at Madison Square Garden, 1979.

With the advent of a new decade, Springsteen then continued to concentrate his thematic focus on working-class life and further cemented his status as a recording artist with his fifth studio record. Released on October 10th 1980, *The River* was a 20-song, double-album heavyweight, which included an intentionally paradoxical range of material

from good-time party rockers to emotionally intense ballads, and finally yielded Springsteen's first Top Ten hit single as a performer, *Hungry Heart*. The two-LP monster constituted a notable shift in Springsteen's style towards an accessible, user-friendly pop-rock sound that was all but missing from any of his earlier work. This was apparent in the stylistic adoption of

certain 80s pop-rock hallmarks like the reverberating tenor drums, very basic percussion/guitar and repetitive lyrics apparent in many of the tracks. And while the haunting title song pointed to the more mature, intellectual course that Springsteen's music was plotting, a couple of the lesser-known tracks presaged his future artistic direction.

The haunting title song pointed to the more mature, intellectual course that Springsteen's music was plotting.

On stage with a lucky fan in London, England, 1981.

The mass-market appeal of *The River* ensured that it sold by the bucket load: 5 million copies flew out of record stores, ensuring Springsteen's first pole position on the Billboard Pop Albums chart, while a long tour promoting the release followed in 1980 and 1981. Those concerts marked the first occasion on which Springsteen played extended dates in Europe and then brought the journey to a grand finale with a series of multi-night arena shows in major U.S. cities. Here, the travelling blueprint for Bruce was firmly set in stone!

Even if one acknowledges the monumental breakthrough impact of *Born to Run*, Springsteen had taken his success to the next level now by winning the vote of the pop-buying public and reaching the cash-cow promised land that lesser artists could only imagine in their dreams. A No. 1 album containing two hits was definitely not to be sniffed at: *Fade Away* entered the Top 40, while the sing-along *Hungry Heart* reached No. 5, introducing Springsteen to a brand new demographic of fans.

New York punk legends The Ramones, pictured in the 1970s.

Following a meeting with New York punk band The Ramones in Asbury Park, Springsteen complied with Joey Ramone's request for a decent song, but then hung on to *Hungry Heart* at the suggestion of his manager, Jon Landau – revealing the street smarts that went hand in hand with his creativity. On the single, Bruce's voice seemed to have mellowed. Was this a deliberate career move to curry favour with American consumers? The delivery seemed dulcet, almost fabricated, the unexpected sweetness evoking memories of Bob Dylan's voice and its new, non-smoking clarity on *Nashville Skyline*. In Springsteen's case, it was in fact the magic box in the studio that produced the iconic fresh sound on the hit single: The Boss's customary growl was accelerated in post-production.

Was this a deliberate career move to curry favour with American consumers?

By contrast, the title track showcased the edgy appeal of Springsteen's vocals, with the self-revelatory, unashamed lyrics displaying rare depth. Bare your soul as a performer, and the audience will respond. The sense of suffering for love on *The River* was palpable, and the faithful lapped up the heartache. As a young teenager at the time, I could only understand the half of it on the radio, but knew almost subliminally what was being hinted at by The Boss. The unavoidable, double-edged sword of womanhood lay in wait round the next corner, and the pain was most definitely in the post:

"Now those memories come back to haunt me
They haunt me like a curse
Is a dream a lie if it don't come true
Or is it something worse?"

Admirably, Springsteen revealed his master touch as a singer/songwriter on the title track, one of his fans' most cherished tunes. While displaying all his emotional cards throughout the soul-baring story, Springsteen suggested that something far more unsettling was hidden beneath the nakedness. Bare your soul, but always preserve one layer of the onion. You might need it one day.

"Glory Days" - a rare shot of Bruce in the early 1970s.

Springsteen's follow-up to *The River* displayed
none of its forerunner's feel-good factor.

Unpredictability will always remain one of the recording artist's strongest suits, and Springsteen revealed this in startling fashion with the 1982 release of his next album, *Nebraska* – his sixth studio work. In the same manner that 1978's *Darkness on the Edge of Town* had provided a meditative contrast to the rip-roaring flamboyance of its predecessor, *Born to Run*, Springsteen's follow-up to *The River* displayed none of its forerunner's feel-good factor.

Following a lengthy period on the road after *The River's* massive success, Springsteen tinkered away on a new collection of songs in more familiar surroundings. Cut by the artist at the studio in his house on a Tascam 4-track tape deck and described as "my ultimate home demo", Springsteen's solo material evidenced his desire to experiment with different styles.

Recording sessions then ensued with The E Street Band to expand

Landau realised that the songs worked better in their stripped-down form than as full-band numbers. Although the recordings of The E Street Band were shelved, other songs from these sessions would later be released, including *Born in the U.S.A.* and *Glory Days*, while Springsteen's original acoustic demo was launched as *Nebraska* on September 20th 1982.

Desolate, stark, and relentlessly bleak in its outlook, this new addition to the Springsteen canon failed to match the impressive sales figures of *Darkness on the Edge of Town* and *The River*. Nevertheless, *Nebraska* still reached the Top Ten and managed to shift a million copies without the assistance of a hit single or a promotional tour in conjunction with its release. Critically, the album received favourable reviews, even though the grim subject matter of Springsteen's lyrics veered into far darker territory than

"Dancing In The Dark", 1981.

Charles Starkweather of Nebraska, pictured after his arrest in 1958.

The best singer/songwriters often challenge themselves with a shift in musical direction.

Nebraska was named Album of the Year by the scribes of *Rolling Stone* magazine and influenced future works by other artists, such as U2's album *The Joshua Tree*. It also helped to inspire the musical genre called lo-fi (i.e. low-fidelity – sound recordings of lower quality than the usual musical standard), and became a cult favourite among indie-rockers.

Apparently in a depressed state when he penned the *Nebraska* material, Springsteen's ten-song end product was a brutal depiction of American life.

The best singer/songwriters often challenge themselves and their hard-won audience with a seismic shift in musical direction, and *Nebraska* was a case in point: menace seemed to be the dish of the day on

this Springsteen menu. The title track spoke of 1950s American 'spree killer' Charlie Starkweather – raised and executed in the Midwestern state of Nebraska and brought to the screen by director Terrence Malick in the 1973 crime drama, *Badlands* – while the spectre of violence seemed to overshadow the romantic façade of *Atlantic City*. You could almost taste the tension.

Once again, Springsteen was peppering his work with real-life imagery, drawing from his seemingly inexhaustible well of personal experience: "This song was about the early-80s gold rush when gambling hit South Jersey." Here was a world far removed from the hit-single jollity of *Hungry Heart*, a coastal resort that reeked of desperation and tawdry makeup. A gaming hellhole

populated by the unsavoury:

"Now there's trouble busin' in from
outta state
And the D.A. can't get no relief
Gonna be a rumble out on the
promenade and
The gamblin' commission's hangin' on
by the skin of its teeth."

Retrospectively, Springsteen's austere, downbeat selection of tracks might have seemed a risky career move at the time, but his radical change of tone on *Nebraska* was vindicated in the main by the album's critical reception. Springsteen's next record would blow his audience out of the water…

"Can't start a fire without a spark" – Bruce in 1981.

With the E Street Band in LA, 1985.

At Giants Stadium during the Born In The USA Tour, 1985.

BORN TO PERFORM

WITHIN A MONTH of its release on June 4th 1984, Springsteen's seventh studio album, *Born in the U.S.A.*, had shifted a million copies. The artist's calling card would go on to sell 10 million by November the following year and a colossal 15 million in the U.S. alone by 1995, guaranteeing its position among the best-selling records of all time.

Every superlative applies to this money-printing colossus of the 1980s. Its pedigree goes unchallenged and confirmed Springsteen's place amongst rock's elite, while elevating him simultaneously to pop-royalty status alongside Michael Jackson and Prince. *Born in the U.S.A.* hit the No. 1 spot worldwide, boasted one of the decade's most abiding pop-culture images on its front cover by photographer Annie Leibowitz and produced seven Top Ten singles from 12 tracks. Among those chart entries, the autobiographical, tender *My Hometown* and

the playfully nostalgic *Glory Days* still impress.

With regard to two of the additional hits, Springsteen revealed his romantic side on *Cover Me* – originally penned for Donna Summer but retained – while the erotic charge and begging declaration of passion in *I'm on Fire* remain one of The Boss's most poignant moments as a songwriter. This was poetry for the people at its most beguiling, burning a hole through hearts all over the globe in less than three minutes. English teachers of the world, take note, sentiment as beautiful and hypnotic as this should take pride of place on any national curriculum:

> "At night I wake up with the sheets soaking wet
> And a freight train running through the Middle of my head
> Only you can cool my desire
> I'm on fire"

On stage at Washington DC's RFK Stadium, 1985.

As for the album's incendiary title track, which kicked off the action like a whirlwind, this was the moment for Springsteen's artistic credo to blaze out of him: "When you get the music and the lyrics right, your voice disappears into the voices of those you've chosen to write about... But all the telling detail in the world doesn't matter if the song lacks an emotional centre."

There was an emotional centre, for sure, in the singer's bitter commentary on the treatment of Vietnam veterans in America, although the genesis of Springsteen's signature tune was more of a happy accident than an original mission statement. The artist explains: "In 1981, director Paul Schrader sent me a script called *Born in the U.S.A.* He wanted me to come up with some music for the film. But the script sat on my writing table until one day I was singing a new song I was writing called Vietnam. I looked over and sang off the top of Paul's cover page: 'I was born in the U.S.A.'"

"All the telling detail in the world doesn't matter if the song lacks an emotional centre"

The Los Angeles Memorial Colisseum, 1985.

The Born In The USA Tour, Giants Stadium, NJ, 1985

Sometimes you have to take a stand for your principles. He wasn't in the game just for the money.

Hollywood legend Schrader was no stranger to the Vietnam issue (in 1976, his career-defining screenplay *Taxi Driver* had dealt explicitly with the emotional breakdown of a disturbed Vietnam vet on the mean streets of New York), but his *Born in the U.S.A.* subject matter was destined for a different medium this time. Taking his musical inspiration from Schrader's screenplay, Springsteen wrote the intended film's title track but was so satisfied with it that he kept the song for the future. In its place, he came up with a different composition for the writer/director called *Light of Day*. This would become the new title of Schrader's film when it reached the screen in 1987, starring Michael J Fox as a Cleveland factory employee who moonlights in a band.

But with Springsteen's voice of authority stamped all over Schrader's initial material, *Born in the U.S.A.* would become the singer's personal tribute to those who had fallen in the Vietnam conflict, as well as a savage indictment of an aggressive U.S. foreign policy:

"Got in a little hometown jam so they put a rifle in my hand
Sent me off to a foreign land to go and kill the yellow man"

Often misunderstood as an endorsement of Republican values at the time, Springsteen's most memorable single was completely misappropriated by then-President Ronald Reagan during his landslide re-election campaign in 1984. Seemingly perfect for political rallies or a unified stadium experience on home soil,

Born in the U.S.A. was adopted as a mantra by many, a far cry from the raging condemnation intended by its creator. And in its incarnation as a live-show spectacular, the emotional anthem encouraged jingoistic flag-waving en masse, even though the lyrics underlined the dangers of America policing the world, the threat of post-war unemployment for Vietnam service personnel and the 'long-gone' horror of post-traumatic stress disorder. Even the Chrysler Corporation jumped on the *Born...* bandwagon, offering The Boss several million dollars for the use of his song in a car advertisement. Bruce turned them down. Sometimes you have to take a stand for your principles. He wasn't in the game just for the money. But he was definitely one hell of a "cool-rocking daddy in the U.S.A."

The 1984 US election saw Reagan re-elected with the most electoral votes ever received.

Away from all the politicisation and misguided patriotism of his album's title song, Springsteen picked up his first Grammy Award for Best Male Rock Vocal Performance with the radio-friendly *Dancing in the Dark*. The most successful of the 7 Top Ten singles generated by *Born in the U.S.A.*, it peaked at No. 2 on the Billboard charts, and still represents the highest position achieved by Springsteen with one of his own compositions. Though hard to believe, The Boss has never managed a No. 1 hit single for himself.

Dancing in the Dark paraded a confident, attractive Springsteen with heart on sleeve, but the catchy refrain and punchy, up-tempo rhythm of this chart blaster were propelling a more complex story. How ironic that the distracted singer was dealing here with the weightier issue of creative stagnation, the millstone of writer's block threatening to drown the artist in search of a hit:

"I'm dying for some action
I'm sick of sitting 'round here trying to
write this book
I need a love reaction
Come on now baby gimme just one look"

Consistent appearances of the song on MTV saw the power of television bringing Bruce to a brand new audience. And on one unforgettable occasion in New York, the newly crowned teen idol was mobbed for his autograph by an adoring gaggle of Catholic schoolgirls! The rest of us can only dream…

The accompanying video for *Dancing in the Dark* was shot in Minnesota at the opening show of The Born in the U.S.A. Tour (a 15-month extravaganza from North America to Australasia, Europe and back between June 29th 1984 and October 2nd 1985). Long before her fame in *Friends* and the *Scream* film franchise, actress Courteney Cox enjoyed her bit part as a glittery-eyed fan dancing with Bruce on stage, and – prophetically for some – Brian De Palma directed. A year earlier in his explosive gangster drama *Scarface*, the words THE WORLD IS YOURS had heralded the rise to power of lead character Tony Montana (Al Pacino) in the Miami night. And for Springsteen now in 1984, the world really was his as *Born in the U.S.A.* began touring the globe.

After 3 months on the road, The Boss's visibility in the press and popular culture was at an unprecedented level. Standing at the summit of his career, he would soon play his part in events that attracted frenzied media attention.

A hometown gig at The Meadowlands, New Jersey, 1984.

On stage with Patti and the band, Giants Stadium, 1985.

The USA For Africa recording session, January 1985. Bruce can be seen in the front row between Cyndi Lauper and James Ingram.

Lionel Richie, Elizabeth Taylor, Michael Jackson and more join together to sing *We Are The World*.

The London Live Aid concert at Wembley Stadium, July 13th 1985.

The event was one of the largest-scale satellite link-ups and TV broadcasts of all time.

In October 1984, a BBC report in the UK highlighted the famine that was blighting Ethiopia. In response, Irish singer Bob Geldof and Midge Ure of Ultravox came up with the idea of a money-raising single entitled *Do They Know It's Christmas?* A month later, Geldof put together a group called Band Aid, consisting of leading British and Irish musicians who were among the most popular of the era. On 25th November 1984, Geldof and Ure's song for famine relief was recorded in London and released four days later. *Do They Know It's Christmas?* became the biggest-selling single in UK Singles Chart history at the time, shifting a million copies in the first week alone. It stayed at No. 1 for five weeks, was the Christmas No. 1, and sold more than 3.5 million copies domestically. Following the song's record-breaking sales in aid of the Ethiopian crisis, Geldof then set his sights on staging a huge concert, 1985's Live Aid, to raise further funds.

The United States were keen to show their support, and quickly followed suit. On the back of Band Aid's *Do They Know It's Christmas?* success in the UK, an idea for the creation of an American benefit single and album for African famine aid came from activist Harry Belafonte. He, along with fundraiser Ken Kragen, was instrumental in bringing the vision to reality. Michael Jackson and Lionel Richie were assigned the task of writing the song, while Quincy Jones and Michael Omartian oversaw its production. Richie and Jackson completed their creation *We Are the World* in early 1985. Under the banner of the assembled group USA for Africa, the song was recorded on January 28th. Springsteen was among the luminaries of the American music establishment that participated in the charity project, delivering his growling vocals with all the passion that he could muster

We Are the World was released on March 7th 1985, as the only single from the album of the same name. A global triumph with sales in excess of 20 million copies, it topped music charts throughout the world and became the fastest-selling American pop single in history. As well as being the first ever single to receive a multi-platinum certification, *We Are the World* received a hatful of honours: three Grammy Awards, one American Music Award and a People's Choice Award. It was promoted with a well-received music video and a range of merchandise, raising over $63 million for humanitarian aid in Africa and the U.S. In addition to the title track, the album included nine previously unreleased songs by donating artists, including Tina Turner and Prince. Playing his part for the cause in tandem with The E Street Band, Springsteen contributed a rendition of Jimmy Cliff's *Trapped*. Recorded live at Meadowlands Arena on The Born in the U.S.A. Tour, the song achieved considerable album-oriented rock-radio airplay, reaching the No. 1 spot on the Billboard Top Rock Tracks chart.

Despite his laudable contribution to both the single and album of *We Are the World* at the beginning of 1985, Springsteen's involvement with the Live Aid concerts that followed in the summer was a different matter altogether.

Orchestrated by Bob Geldof and Midge Ure to raise funds on behalf of the ongoing Ethiopian famine – with the sterling support of music promoter Harvey Goldsmith – the dual-venue marathon took place on July 13th 1985. Billed as the global jukebox, Live Aid was held simultaneously at Wembley Stadium in London and Philadelphia's JFK Stadium in the United States. On the same day, concerts inspired by the initiative occurred in Australia and Germany. The event was one of the largest-scale satellite link-ups and TV broadcasts of all time: an estimated total audience of 1.9 billion tuned in.

Freddie Mercury and Queen were among the performers to receive a huge commercial boost from their Live Aid appearances.

Taking into consideration Springsteen's sympathy for worthy causes, it may come as something of a surprise that he declined an invitation by Geldof to play at Live Aid's Wembley concert. The singer/songwriter stated at a later date that he "simply did not realise how big the whole thing was going to be" (figures would have it that the charity event raised £150 million). And Springsteen has also expressed regret since at turning down Geldof's call-up, explaining that he could have played a couple of acoustic songs had there been no slot available for a full-band performance. Even if one accepts that Springsteen had already reached his broadest audience demographic on The Born in the U.S.A. Tour, in purely cynical self-promotion terms Live Aid would have launched him into a new galaxy as a recording artist (whether intentionally or not, David Bowie, Queen and U2 all benefited from their stupendous Live Aid performances at Wembley).

Live Aid would have launched him into a new galaxy as a recording artist.

Bruce's first wife Julianne Phillips, pictured in 2007.

But if you analyse the bare bones of Springsteen's professional and personal schedule from October 1984 to July 1985, the combined pieces of the jigsaw offer some explanation for his absence from Live Aid. During The Born in the U.S.A. Tour in October 1984, Springsteen met his first spouse, actress-and-model Julianne Phillips. In the interim between the Australasian and European legs of the tour, the couple were married on May 13th 1985. Springsteen then returned to work on June 1st, performing a gig at Slane Castle in Ireland that has deservedly entered rock 'n' roll folklore. This concert was followed, ironically, by three shows at Wembley Stadium before the European Springsteen experience came to a close at Roundhay Park in Leeds on July 7th 1985 – barely a week before Live Aid. Irrespective of his regrets (after the event), one can only assume that a combination of exhaustion, unwavering media attention and a loving wife to concentrate on forced Springsteen to stay away. There was also the fourth and final leg of his tour to complete, the emotional North American homecoming that would commence in Washington on August 5th. Ultimately, whatever The Boss's motivation was for not doing Live Aid, his English fans could only wonder what the occasion might have been like with his inclusion. Would he have trumped the other acts to produce the defining performance of the day?

Fans at Live Aid try to keep cool, London 1985.

Live/1975-85 on sale in New York City, 1986.

EMOTIONAL TURMOIL

AFTER THE EXERTIONS of a 15-month road show with The Born in the U.S.A. Tour, Springsteen needed time for rest and introspection. The artist explains the reasons behind this period of respite: "After '85 I'd had enough: I turned inward to write about men, women and love, things that had previously been on the periphery of my work." Release-wise, this second part of the decade gave Springsteen the opportunity to repackage the

glories of his past, and to reacquaint his fans with some of his most spectacular concerts – a crucial component of his personal and singer/songwriting identity. At the end of November 1986 (the year that saw Springsteen win the British Phonographic Industry Award for International Solo Artist), he released the retrospective collection *Live/1975-85.*

Exploiting Springsteen's reputation as a virtuoso live performer, this five-LP/three-

cassette/three-CD box set summed up Springsteen's career to that point and displayed some of the elements that made his shows so powerful to his loyal audience: the switching from mournful dirges to party rockers and back; the communal sense of purpose between artist and fan; the long, spoken passages before songs, including those that described Springsteen's difficult relationship with his father; and the prowess

Live/1975-85 remains one of the most profitable live albums of all time.

of The E Street Band.

Live/1975-85 arrived in the American album charts in the No. 1 slot and became the first box set to debut at the top. It produced a Top Ten hit with a cover version of *War* (originally by Edwin Starr) and, with extraordinary U.S. sales figures of 13 million copies, remains one of the most profitable live albums of all time.

In stark contrast to its predecessor, the next release from Springsteen was a studio-bound, introverted piece of work. Launched on the market on October 9th 1987, the 12-track *Tunnel of Love* revealed the more vulnerable aspects of the singer's character. As Springsteen approached 40 and his marriage to Julianne Phillips disintegrated, his personal turmoil came to the fore on the album, but the candid self-exposure had universal appeal for the audience.

The release of *Tunnel of Love* was delayed to avoid clashing with Michael Jackson's *Bad*.

Like its studio forerunner *Born in the U.S.A.*, *Tunnel of Love* sailed into the American charts at No. 1, shifting 3 million units in the process. Songs from this sedate collection about the tribulations of love found favour with the single-buying public as well. *One Step Up* reached the Top 40, while the title track and *Brilliant Disguise* achieved Top Ten status. As for the album's critical reception, it won Springsteen his second Male Rock Vocal Grammy.

A husband for barely two and a half years at the time of *Tunnel of Love's* release, Springsteen's lengthy periods on the road would eventually seal the end of his first marriage. He became close to backing vocalist Patti Scialfa after the latter's introduction to The Born in the U.S.A. Tour in 1984, and the pair's subsequent affair was the final straw for Julianne Phillips.

Maybe every poet needs the pain, because the emotional fallout between Phillips and Springsteen found a perfect outlet in the singer's material, even though

the random nature of love could not be explained simplistically: "Adult life is dealing with an enormous amount of questions that don't have answers. So I let the mystery settle into my music. I don't deny anything, I don't advocate anything – I just live with it."

On the album's most memorable track, *Brilliant Disguise*, the eternal mysteries of attraction provided the song's heartbeat. Here, Springsteen's growing maturity allowed for unabashed self-analysis, as he questioned his own romantic choices. Was his first wife the appropriate lady for him, or merely a source of unhappiness?

"I heard somebody call your name
From underneath our willow
I saw something tucked in shame
Underneath your pillow
Well I've tried so hard baby
But I just can't see
What a woman like you
Is doing with me"

On stage with Patti in East Berlin, 1988.

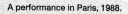
A performance in Paris, 1988.

Revealing his depth as well as his artistic dexterity on keyboards, bass, vocals and guitar, Springsteen continued to cast the spell with *Brilliant Disguise*. Here he was again, like *The River*, baring his soul to listeners, yet still preserving that one layer of the onion. Not everything was clear.

The suitability of his spouse may have been questioned in full view of the world, as the recurring themes of fidelity and insecurity rose inexorably to the surface. But after pondering throughout the song whether his love had been wearing a mask all along, Springsteen wondered, in the perfect twist, if he himself might be the dark horse of the relationship. The pay-off was delicious, the sign of a master storyteller at work:

"So when you look at me
You better look hard and look twice

Is that me baby
Or just a brilliant disguise?"

Tunnel of Love constituted Springsteen's fourth No. 1-selling American album during the 1980s, and in February 1988 The Tunnel of Love Express Tour hit the road to support the record. In May of that year, Springsteen and Julianne Phillips separated, after which the singer started living with Patti Scialfa. Phillips then filed for divorce in August 1988, and amid a storm of press criticism for the hastiness in which he and Scialfa began cohabiting, Springsteen escaped the invasion into his personal life by headlining the six-week Human Rights Now! Tour. As well as The E Street Band, Tracy Chapman, Peter Gabriel and Sting showed their humanitarian side by joining this worldwide benefit for Amnesty International.

Springsteen escaped the invasion into his personal life by headlining a six-week tour.

With Sting in Paris for the Human Rights Now! Tour, 1988.

Accomplished equestrian Jessica Springsteen competing at the Royal Windsor Horse Show, 2011.

An impromptu gig at LA's China Club with Don Henley of The Eagles (left) and Sting, 1990.

As the 1980s came to a close, Springsteen retreated from the public gaze in a bid to settle down with his new love, Patti Scialfa, and find a modicum of peace. He was divorced from Julianne Phillips in March 1989 and then dissolved The E Street Band (temporarily) in November. On July 25th the following year, Scialfa gave birth to her first child with Springsteen, Evan James. Next, the adoring couple cemented their union officially on June 8th 1991 when they tied the knot at their new home in Beverly Hills. Jessica 'Jesse' Rae Springsteen became the second addition to the family on December 30th 1991.

Having settled into fatherhood for the first time, Springsteen gave evidence of his Californian creativity with the simultaneous release of two albums in March 1992. Featuring a selection of new session musicians as the singer's backup band, both *Human Touch* and *Lucky Town* enjoyed considerable success, even though they were less outgoing in nature than The Boss's two works prior to *Tunnel of Love*. Showcasing fresh levels of confidence from Springsteen, the dual releases stormed into the charts at numbers two and three respectively, with *Human Touch* being the more popular of the two, eventually hitting the coveted UK No. 1 position. Each achieved platinum status, and the double-sided single that paired *Human Touch* with *Lucky Town's* opening track *Better Days* was a Top 40 hit. The latter song, in particular, illustrated a moment when Springsteen had attained emotional and artistic peace with two children and a beautiful wife, even though *Human Touch* and *Lucky Town* had failed to match the triple-platinum commercial pedigree of *Tunnel of Love*. The man himself recalls the period fondly: "I was feelin' like a happy guy who has his rough days rather than vice versa."

At this stage of his life, Springsteen seemed unfazed by criticism in some quarters of the media about his relocation to Tinseltown and his adoption of a different backing band. There were concerns that the New Jersey boy had betrayed both his regular group of musicians and his gritty background by moving to the 'plastic' paradise of Los Angeles.

Maybe the poet does need
the pain of emotional
turmoil to produce
his finest work.

On stage in Stockholm, 1993.

Bruce and Patti, Frankfurt 1988.

Did these joyous times indicate a mellow new identity and musical approach for Springsteen? His electric band appearance in September 1992 on MTV's (normally) acoustic *Unplugged* show seemed to suggest a more rebellious return to old form, but when the latter concert surfaced (as the album *In Concert/MTV Plugged*) on April 12th 1993, it received a lukewarm reception. Springsteen appeared to acknowledge the shortcomings of this LA era when he spoke amusingly about his deceased father during his Rock and Roll Hall of Fame acceptance speech in 1999: "I've gotta thank him because… what would I conceivably have written about without him? I mean, you can imagine that if everything had gone great between us, we would have had disaster. I would have written just happy songs… and I tried it in the early 90s and it didn't work; the public didn't like

it." Maybe the poet does need the pain of emotional turmoil to produce his finest work, and maybe Springsteen's adoring core audience wanted the customary strength of his earlier material. Two factors were certain, though: Springsteen couldn't please everyone all of the time, and he was satisfied with himself and with life in the City of Angels. Samuel Ryan Springsteen brought further contentment to Bruce and Patti Scialfa when he was born in Los Angeles on January 5th 1994. Nevertheless, Springsteen remained upset by the initial press reaction to his involvement with Scialfa. Interviewed in 1995, he spoke passionately about the negative publicity that he and his new wife had had to endure from the media's self-righteous moral guardians: "It's a strange society that assumes it has the right to tell people whom they should love and whom

they shouldn't. But the truth is, I basically ignored the entire thing as much as I could. I said: 'Well, all I know is, this feels real, and maybe I have got a mess going here in some fashion, but that's life.'" He also noted that: "I went through a divorce, and it was really difficult and painful and I was very frightened about getting married again. So part of me said: 'Hey, what does it matter?' But it does matter. It's very different than just living together. First of all, stepping up publicly – which is what you do: you get your licence, you do all the social rituals – is a part of your place in society and in some way part of society's acceptance of you. Patti and I both found that it did mean something." It still does mean something. Almost 21 years after they gained 'acceptance' by tying the knot, Springsteen and Scialfa are still married. Love conquers all.

Bruce playing with one of his idols, Bob Dylan,
at the Rock 'n' Roll Hall of Fame, 1995.

Elvis Presley was certainly no stranger to cross-marketing. Jailhouse Rock, pictured, was a successful movie as well as a hit record.

The silver screen played a major role in shaping the singer's identity.

AT THE

ALTHOUGH MUSIC WAS always Springsteen's primary source of inspiration, the silver screen played a major role in shaping the singer's identity. As he grew up in 1950s America, the movie-making epicentre of the world acted as the ideal breeding ground for a fertile imagination. John Ford's classic western *The Searchers* (1956) intrigued Springsteen as a boy, and his love of cinema grew. Later on, the early influence of the medium would be translated into the songwriter's music: apart from the obvious nod to Robert Mitchum's *Thunder Road* on *Born to Run*, Springsteen derived inspiration from John Ford's 1940 saga *The Grapes of Wrath* for his 1995 album *The Ghost of Tom Joad*, while director Louis Malle's atmospheric *Atlantic City* (1980) appeared in 1982 with the Springsteen signature in his mournful *Nebraska*.

Elsewhere in the movie world, Springsteen's style has added to the texture of other artists' work. Firstly, the singer's compositions have decorated a smorgasbord of soundtracks: the earliest appearance of Springsteen songs seems to have been on the 1982 prostitution drama *Dead End Street*, while the Tom Cruise money-spinners *Risky Business* (1983) and *Jerry Maguire* (1996) also delivered The Boss to a cinematic audience. The 'cross-marketing' potential of such exercises is limitless in commercial terms, and Springsteen has often been the perfect 'fit' for a particular movie: by complementing a film – on the trailer, for example – a Springsteen song can 'make' a picture. The song sells the movie, and the movie sells the song. Elvis Presley, one of cross-marketing's founding fathers, would certainly be proud of his 'boy'.

MOVIES

With actor Mickey Rourke at the 2009 Golden Globe Awards.

Director Thom Zimny with his 2007 Grammy Award for
Wings For Wheels: The Making Of Born To Run.

Springsteen has fuelled the creative fire of others with his music.

Secondly, Springsteen has enhanced the movies of others either by writing songs specifically for them or by appearing on screen, often at an actor or director's behest. If you want talent, avoid the middleman and go straight to The Boss! For instance, Springsteen played himself in a short cameo in the comedy drama *High Fidelity* (2000) and composed the brooding, Oscar-nominated *Dead Man Walkin'* for the 1995 death-row drama *Dead Man Walking*. Also, his Golden Globe-winning song for *The Wrestler* (2008) came to fruition after a pleading letter from the film's star, Mickey Rourke. Director Darren Aronofsky loved the end product: "Bruce Springsteen wrote a beautiful original song for the closing of the film. Called *The Wrestler*, it is a wonderful acoustic piece. Makes me choke up every time I hear it. He really captured the spirit of the film and

Mickey's character in the piece."

Thirdly, apart from boosting a film's impact with the use of his recorded or original material, Springsteen has fuelled the creative fire of others with his music. Director Walter Hill's 1984 fantasy thriller *Streets of Fire* took its name from the song of the same name on Springsteen's album *Darkness on the Edge of Town*, while American actor Sean Penn wrote and directed his first film *The Indian Runner* (1991) as a tribute of sorts to Springsteen's *Nebraska* track *Highway Patrolman*. Additionally, a documentary about the making of the singer's *Darkness* album was premiered at the Toronto International Film Festival in September 2010. Entitled *The Promise: The Making of Darkness on the Edge of Town*, director Thom Zimny's work examined Springsteen's role in the production of his fourth studio record.

Despite the inspiration that he provided for his film-world admirers, it was one of Springsteen's own creations that proved the most inspirational. And in the 1993 movie *Philadelphia*, he reached the pinnacle of his craft. Oscar-winning director Jonathan Demme (*The Silence of the Lambs*) required a song to suit the mood of his new project: Springsteen was the man to call.

Hot on the heels of the 1993 made-for-cable drama *And the Band Played On*, *Philadelphia* marked the first full-scale attempt by Hollywood to tackle the potentially inflammatory issues of Aids and homosexuality. Shaped to some degree by the 1987 story of Geoffrey Bowers – an attorney who sued the law firm Baker & McKenzie for wrongful dismissal in one of the first Aids-discrimination cases – the movie set a precedent in mainstream film. From here, gay and lesbian characters would be depicted more realistically.

Actor Tom Hanks was signed up to give Demme's TriStar blockbuster the appropriate sensitivity in the role of Andrew Beckett, a hotshot gay attorney who is wrongfully sacked for 'incompetence' when his serpentine bosses notice a lesion on his forehead. Denzel Washington provided the perfect foil to Hanks' HIV-positive Beckett in the part of Joe Miller, a homophobic but street-smart personal-injury lawyer who comes to realise that Beckett's termination is bigoted – and unlawful. "No one would take on his case… Until one man was willing to take on the system," screamed the publicity material, and in the accomplished hands of screenwriter Ron Nyswaner, the resulting drama transcended its setting to become a treatise on humanity.

Springsteen's contribution was crucial. As the film opened with a sweeping montage of city life, his soulful ballad added its heart-rending lyrics to the top-notch production's feel. Springsteen seemed to be carrying the burden for all of us as his voice walked in the shoes of a dying man; his appeal for tolerance and compassion sounded more like a hymn as it soared beyond the confines of the film-bound setting.

Philadelphia star Tom Hanks with his Best Actor Oscar.

Springsteen seemed to be carrying the burden for all of us.

Co-star Denzel Washington would have to wait until 2002 to receive his first Best Actor Oscar, for the film *Training Day*.

We may have been treading the *Streets of Philadelphia* visually, but emotionally we were wrapped up in Springsteen as he reached out to embrace all the lost souls of the world. Here were noble sentiments that paraded the picture's integrity from the very first frames:

"The night has fallen, I'm lyin' awake
I can feel myself fading away
So receive me brother with your faithless kiss

Or will we leave each other alone like this
On the streets of Philadelphia?"

The dynamic interplay of Springsteen, Demme and ace cinematographer Tak Fujimoto – as well as sensational performances by Hanks and Washington – pressed all the right critical and commercial buttons. *Philadelphia* grossed $77,446,440 in the US and $129,232,000 overseas, totalling $206,678,440. It was a massive success, and became the 12th highest-grossing film in the US for 1993. It received Academy

Bruce with Whitney Houston and his Oscar for Best Original Song, 1994.

Award nominations for Best Original Song (Neil Young for *Philadelphia*) and Best Makeup (Carl Fullerton and Alan D'Angerio). Screenwriter Ron Nyswaner was also in the running for a statuette alongside Gary Ross for *Dave*, but both lost out to Jane Campion for *The Piano*.

Hanks won his first Best Actor Oscar for his portrayal of a man ravaged by Aids, beating Liam Neeson (*Schindler's List*) and Anthony Hopkins (*The Remains of the Day*) to the gong. Hanks also won the Silver Bear for Best Actor at the Berlin International Film Festival, and the Golden Globe. A year later, he repeated his Oscar-Globe double for *Forrest Gump*.

As for Mr Springsteen, the magnificent *Streets of Philadelphia* won him the Academy Award for Best Original Song. "Thanks for inviting me to your party!" he declared with characteristic humour during his Oscar acceptance speech. The recording also became a Top Ten hit, winning four Grammys, including Song of the Year and Best Rock Song. It was a major coup, and all the accolades for *Streets of Philadelphia* were merited. As Hanks' character put it poignantly to Washington's in the film: "Excellent work, counsellor."

With guitar legend Chuck Berry at the Rock 'n' Roll Hall Of Fame, 1995.

Clutching his haul of four Grammys at the 1995 awards show.

The haunting *Secret Garden* provided *Greatest Hits* with one of its most murky and luxurious moments.

MR MAJ

PROFITING FROM THE stability engendered by the birth of his third child in 1994, Bruce Springsteen celebrated the past once more within twelve months of Samuel's arrival. In early 1995, The Boss's 18-track *Greatest Hits* collection set his legend in stone with its eclectic overview of standards from the past twenty years. Comparable in scope to the release of *Live/1975-85* a decade before, this compendium of career-defining gems summarised Springsteen's undoubted abilities as a studio hit-maker. *Streets of Philadelphia* worked its magic in the company of old favourites such as *Thunder Road* and *Atlantic City* on the album, while Springsteen bolstered the material with four new tracks that re-united The E Street Band. It was a formula that could not fail.

Grammy-nominated documentarist Ernie Fritz captured The E Street Band sessions in his 1996 film, *Blood Brothers*. From these group recordings, the haunting *Secret Garden* provided *Greatest Hits* with one of its most murky – and luxurious – moments. Recalling Springsteen's desire in 1985 to focus creatively on the themes of women and love, the song delivered one of the artist's most hypnotic performances.

Here, Springsteen spun the story of an

ESTIC

inscrutable woman who inspired adoration for sure, but fear by association.

Accompanied by the slinky piano of long-time E Street collaborator Roy Bittan, the mellifluous vocals introduced listeners to the definitive femme fatale of film noir. Forget the happy-go-lucky dancing Mary from the Robert Mitchum-inspired *Thunder Road*. 20 years on, here was a lady more akin to a black widow, or lovely Jane Greer suckering poor old patsy Bob Mitchum

down the road to ruin in *Out of the Past*:

"She'll look at you and smile
And her eyes will say
She's got a secret garden
Where everything you want
Where everything you need
Will always stay
A million miles away"

A year after the quadruple-platinum glory

of *Greatest Hits*, *Secret Garden*'s bankability was enhanced further by its appearance in the Tom Cruise-Renée Zellweger slush fest, *Jerry Maguire*. Re-released in 1997, this dazzling pearl from *Greatest Hits* became a Top 40 hit, climbing eventually to No. 19 on the Billboard Hot 100. Springsteen was absolutely raking it in at this point: even if he'd had us at "hello" with *Secret Garden*, he had no need (unlike *Jerry Maguire* co-star Cuba Gooding Jr) to scream: "Show me the money!"

The Ghost Of Tom Joad solo tour, 1995.

Instead of reconvening The E Street Band at this juncture, Springsteen then released his 2nd (mostly) solo guitar album, *The Ghost of Tom Joad*. Inspired by John Steinbeck's *The Grapes of Wrath* and by *Journey to Nowhere: the Saga of the New Underclass*, a book by Pulitzer Prize-winning author Dale Maharidge and photographer Michael Williamson, the downbeat material raised comparisons with Springsteen's earlier *Nebraska*. Sombre in outlook, the LP won a Grammy for best contemporary folk album, but it missed the Top Ten and only went gold. Critically, Springsteen's near-acoustic effort gained respect for its worthy examination of

immigration and poverty, and the singer hit the road to coincide with the album's release on November 21st 1995. During the next two calendar years, Springsteen's solo Ghost of Tom Joad Tour visited a series of small venues worldwide: the minimalist sets showcased a variety of Springsteen favourites in stripped-down, acoustic form. Before the gigs ended in Paris on May 26th 1997, Springsteen took a diversion to Stockholm, where he received the Royal Swedish Academy of Music's most prestigious award, the Polar Music Prize. Such uninterrupted activity must have played a part in shaping the singer's plans for the future.

Springsteen's near-acoustic effort gained respect for its worthy examination of immigration and poverty.

Success at the tills
confirmed Springsteen's
majestic position
in the marketplace.

In Stockholm to receive the Polar Music prize, 1997. Eric Ericson
(right) shared the prize for his work in classical music.

In the latter part of the last millennium, Springsteen returned to New Jersey with his family in a bid to escape the LA spotlight. His father died in 1998, the year that prompted the artist to take stock of the past by introducing his back catalogue to a new generation: on November 10th, Springsteen released the four-CD box set *Tracks*. This monumental retrospective of previously unreleased material from the early 1970s to the 1990s acknowledged his unquestionable prowess as a singer/songwriter. Platinum success at the tills confirmed Springsteen's majestic position in the marketplace, while his place in the pantheon was confirmed by induction into the Rock and Roll Hall of Fame in January 1999. U2's Bono delivered the ceremonial speech, a favour that Springsteen would return for the band at their 2005 induction.

My City of Ruins would come to symbolise the devastation of New York.

With soul legend Wilson Pickett in New York, 1999.

Having engaged all the 1974-1989 E Street Band line-up for a performance at his Rock and Roll Hall of Fame induction, Springsteen then proved both his durability and loyalty by going on the road again. The leviathan Reunion Tour rolled into action on April 9th 1999, with guitarists Steve Van Zandt and Nils Lofgren both getting the call-up. Springsteen took a break from the European leg of the road show to be inducted into the Songwriters Hall of Fame in June. As his fiftieth birthday approached, the award endorsed just how far the New Jersey boy had come, but age was no barrier to the artist's stamina. The Reunion Tour comprised more than 100 concerts, including a sold-out, 15-show stint at Continental Airlines Arena in East Rutherford, New Jersey and a ten-night sell-out at New York City's Madison Square Garden. Winding down at the latter venue in July 2000, the final two dates of the Springsteen extravaganza surfaced for posterity the following year as *Bruce Springsteen & The E Street Band: Live in New York City*. Launched onto the market on March 27th 2001, the album version of the concerts made the Top

The Rising Tour, London 2002.

Ten and went platinum, and a double DVD followed in November.

Never one to skirt life's darker issues, Springsteen enraptured the critics and the public with his next offering. Released by Columbia records on July 30th 2002 and produced by Brendan O'Brien, *The Rising* constituted the singer's first studio album with the complete line-up of The E Street Band since *Born in the U.S.A.* 18 years of creative separation in no way diminished the power of material that was generally interpreted as Springsteen's response to 9/11.

Containing songs that reflected on the tragedy, *The Rising's* closing track, *My City of Ruins*, would come to symbolise the devastation of New York; originally, though, Springsteen had written it in recognition of the attempts to regenerate the city of Asbury Park in his native New Jersey. Prior to the terrorist atrocities, the singer had advocated Asbury Park's revitalisation, playing an annual series of winter holiday concerts there to support various local businesses, organisations and causes.

But needing an appropriate tune for a post-9/11 benefit concert in honour of New York City, he selected *My City of Ruins*, which was immediately recognised as an emotional highlight of the occasion, with its gospel themes and the rousing entreaties to "rise up!" As a result, the song became associated with post-9/11 New York, and Springsteen chose it to end the album and as an encore on The Rising Tour.

Fittingly, many of *The Rising*'s 15 tracks were inspired by conversations Springsteen had with family members of some of the victims, who stated in their loved ones' obituaries how much The Boss's music had touched their lives. The title song featured prominently on the radio, and the No. 1 record became Springsteen's most successful album of new material for 15 years, selling 2 million copies.

After an early-morning slot on *The Today Show* in Asbury Park – a favourite pre-tour rehearsal location for Springsteen – The Rising

Springsteen's impassioned meditation on loss, hope and faith won him a Grammy for Best Rock Album.

The Rising Tour, Paris 2003.

Tour commenced, barnstorming through a series of single-night arena stands in the U.S. and Europe to promote the album in 2002, then returning for large-scale, multiple-night stadium shows in 2003. While Springsteen had maintained a loyal hardcore fan base everywhere (and particularly in Europe), his general popularity had dipped over the years in some Southern and Midwestern regions of the U.S. But it was still strong in Europe and along the U.S. coasts, and he played an unprecedented 10 nights in Giants Stadium in New Jersey, a ticket-selling feat to which no other musical act has come close. The Rising Tour came to a glorious finale on October 4th 2003, after three nights in Shea Stadium that included a guest appearance by Bob Dylan. As for *The Rising's* performance at the awards, Springsteen's impassioned meditation on loss, hope and faith won him a Grammy for Best Rock Album, while the title track won for Rock Song and Male Rock Vocal.

With The E Street Band, New York's Shea Stadium, 2003.

Even in
his fifties,
The Boss
managed
to maintain
his energy.

On stage with Patti and Steve, London 2002.

UP TO DATE

AS THE NOUGHTIES progressed, Springsteen showed no visible signs of slowing down. Even in his fifties, The Boss managed to maintain his energy, and the years that followed *The Rising's* success were characterised by new studio output and an impressively busy touring schedule. Guest

appearances occurred during this period, too: at the 2003 Grammy Awards, Springsteen performed The Clash's *London Calling* with Elvis Costello, Dave Grohl, Steve Van Zandt and No Doubt bassist Tony Kanal in tribute to the late Joe Strummer. For many, this was a respectful moment as Springsteen and

The Clash had been deemed multiple-album rivals in the days of double-LP *The River* and the 3-LP *Sandinista!* (a case of 'combat rock', if ever there was one).

Further delights maintained Springsteen's positive profile. On November 11th 2003, the artist

Performing with **REM's Michael Stipe** on the Vote For Change tour, 2004.

The following year, Springsteen dipped his foot into political waters.

issued a 3-CD compilation of greatest hits that spanned his entire career. *The Essential Bruce Springsteen* was backed up the week after by *Bruce Springsteen & The E Street Band: Live in Barcelona* (DVD), the first time that a whole Springsteen concert was released on video or audio.

The following year, Springsteen dipped his foot into political waters. In the autumn of 2004, he took part in the Vote for Change concert tour organised to encourage the defeat of George W. Bush in the U.S. presidential election (the effort ultimately failed as Bush was re-elected on

November 2nd 2004).

As well as Springsteen, The E Street Band was present for the proceedings, along with John Mellencamp, John Fogerty, The Dixie Chicks, Pearl Jam, R.E.M., Bright Eyes, The Dave Matthews Band, Jackson Browne and other musicians.

With Democrat candidate John Kerry in Miami, 2004.

All the concerts were to be played in swing states, to benefit the liberal political organisation group America Coming Together and also to encourage people to register and vote. A finale was held in Washington, D.C., bringing many of the artists together. Several days later, Springsteen gave one more such concert in New Jersey, when polls showed that state to be surprisingly close. While in the past Springsteen had played benefits for causes in which he believed – against nuclear energy, for Vietnam veterans, Amnesty International and The Christic Institute – he had always refrained from explicitly promoting candidates for political office (e.g. his rejection of Walter Mondale's attempt to attract an endorsement during the 1984 Reagan *Born in the U.S.A.* era). But his stance in 2004 led to criticism and praise on both sides of the argument. Springsteen's *No Surrender* was used as the key campaign theme song during John Kerry's unsuccessful presidential bid, and during the last days of the Kerry campaign Springsteen performed acoustic versions of the number and some of his other old material at Kerry rallies.

Despite its intimate nature, *Devils & Dust* received the blessing of critical and commercial opinion.

In radical contrast to all the political manoeuvring of 2004, Springsteen was on much less extrovert form with his next piece of studio work. Returning to the downbeat style and mood that had infused both *The Ghost of Tom Joad* and *Nebraska*, the singer released *Devils & Dust*, another solo offering, on April 26th 2005. Recorded without the assistance of The E Street Band, the low key folk album did benefit from some instrumentation but remained a primarily acoustic affair. Despite its intimate nature, *Devils & Dust* received the blessing of critical and commercial opinion. Like its studio predecessor *The Rising*, *Devils & Dust* hit No. 1, entering the album charts of the U.S. and nine other countries in pole position. As well as achieving gold status, the album won Springsteen a Grammy for Best Solo Rock Vocal Performance.

The Devils & Dust solo tour, Oakland 2005.

Some of the songs had been penned almost 10 years before, either during or shortly after The Ghost of Tom Joad Tour; a couple had been performed on the road then but not released. Among the 12 entries on *Devils & Dust*, the emotional title track examined the war in Iraq from a soldier's perspective:

'I've got my finger on the trigger
And tonight faith just ain't enough
When I look inside my heart
There's just devils and dust'

Springsteen took to the road alone to promote the album, kicking off The Devils & Dust Tour on the same day as the disc's release. Between April and November 2005, he played 76 concerts in both small and large venues.

Attendance was disappointing in a few regions, and everywhere (apart from Europe) tickets were more easily obtainable than in the past. Unlike his mid-1990s one-man tour, he performed on a range of instruments other than the guitar, adding variety to the solo

sound. Strange reworkings of *Nebraska's Reason to Believe* and *Darkness on the Edge of Town's The Promised Land* kept the audiences on their toes, while rarities, frequent set-list changes and Springsteen's adoration of performing live ensured a top night out for fans.

Almost a year to the day after the *Devils & Dust* project, Springsteen turned away from an intimate approach for his subsequent studio album. On April 25th 2006, he released *We Shall Overcome: The Seeger Sessions*, a collection of traditional American songs celebrating the radical activism of folk music luminary Pete Seeger (the latter played a prominent role in popularising the spiritual *We Shall Overcome*, the song that became recognised as the anthem of The American Civil Rights Movement during the 1960s). The album was laid down with an ensemble of 18 musicians including Patti Scialfa, Soozie Tyrell and The Miami Horns, a 3-day process that produced hearty material.

Springsteen turned away
from an intimate approach for his
subsequent studio album.

Folk legend Pete Seeger, pictured in 2004.

With The Sessions Band, Chicago 2006.

The Bruce Springsteen with The Seeger Sessions Band Tour began the same month, featuring the musicians known as The Seeger Sessions Band – later abbreviated to The Sessions Band. *Seeger Sessions* songs played constantly on the 7-month road show, as well as a few (usually drastically rearranged) Springsteen numbers. The tour proved very popular in Europe, selling out everywhere and garnering some excellent reviews, but newspapers reported that a number of U.S. shows suffered from sparse attendance. By the end of 2006, The Seeger Sessions Band Tour had been to Europe and back by way of America. The disc *Live in Dublin: Bruce Springsteen with The Sessions Band*, containing the best selections from 3 nights of November 2006 shows at The Point Theatre in Dublin, Ireland, was released on June 5th 2007. The latter album reached the Top 40, while Springsteen's gold-selling *We Shall Overcome…* won him another Grammy – for Best Traditional Folk Album.

Magic cemented his reputation as a recording artist and confirmed his commercial clout.

Back together with
The E Street Band, New York 2007.

Unquestionably, Springsteen had shown his versatility as a singer/songwriter with *We Shall Overcome: The Seeger Sessions*, but his studio follow-up was a spectacular return to form. Released by Columbia Records on October 2nd 2007, *Magic* cemented his reputation as a recording artist and confirmed his commercial clout with its chart-topping success. Marking Springsteen's first studio collaboration with The E Street Band since *The Rising*, and benefiting from the production smarts of Brendan O'Brien, the album served up 11 new Springsteen songs as well as *Long Walk Home*, which had been performed once with The Sessions band. *Magic* debuted at No. 1 on the Billboard chart in America, while reaching the top slot in Ireland and the UK. *Greatest Hits* re-entered the Irish charts at No. 57 during this period, with *Live in Dublin* raising a glass to The Boss as it almost cracked the top 20 in Norway again.

The full Seeger Sessions Band, Asbury Park 2006.

Was there no end to Springsteen's presence in the marketplace? Apparently not, as his high-powered vocal display on the album helped to sell a million units, with the hit single *Radio Nowhere* earning Grammys for Rock Song and Solo Rock Vocal. (Another of *Magic's* gems, the track *Girls in Their Summer Clothes*, would win the Rock Song Grammy the following year.)

Having re-united The E Street Band with the intention of going on the road, The Magic Tour started at the Civic Center in Hartford, Connecticut on the day of the album's release, before progressing through North America and Europe. Springsteen and the band performed live on NBC's *Today Show* in advance of the opener, but the early joy of this 100-show colossus would be overshadowed by sadness. Respected E Street Band member Danny Federici had to take time off in November 2007 to undergo melanoma treatment, and he would eventually succumb to a three-year battle with the disease in April the following year. Federici's unexpected demise caused the first irrevocable change in the group's line-up; he was replaced on tour by Charles Giordano, who had performed with Springsteen previously in The Sessions Band. Later in 2011, saxophonist Clarence Clemons would pass away following a stroke.

When The Magic Tour paused for thought at the end of its first leg in North America in May 2008, Springsteen had the opportunity to attend an amiable awards do. He had been elected to the New Jersey Hall of Fame in 2007 for services to music and entertainment, and an official induction ceremony was now due. On Sunday May 4th 2008, Springsteen was one of 25 inductees at Newark's Performing Arts Center, rubbing shoulders with the Pulitzer Prize-winning novelist Toni Morrison (*Beloved*) and US military icon 'Storming' Norman Schwarzkopf. The occasion delivered some trademark Springsteen showboating: "Rise up, my fellow New Jerseyans. We are all members of a confused but noble race. Even with this wonderful Hall of Fame, we know there's another bad Jersey joke just around the corner!"

He appeared at a number of rallies
and performed several solo acoustic shows to
demonstrate his allegiance.

The Magic Tour ended in August 2008, a time of monumental change in America. Having announced his endorsement of Senator Barack Obama in April 2008, Springsteen supported Obama's presidential campaign when its momentum became unstoppable later that year. He appeared at a number of Obama rallies and performed several solo acoustic shows to demonstrate his allegiance. In Ohio, Springsteen spoke up with passion about the importance of "…truth, transparency and integrity in government, the right of every American to have a job, a living wage, to be educated in a decent school, and to have a life filled with the dignity of work, the promise and the sanctity of home…" He continued: "But today those freedoms have been damaged and curtailed by eight years of a thoughtless, reckless and morally-adrift administration." The culmination of Springsteen's road-show activity was at a rally on November 2nd 2008, where he played material from his new album, *Working on a Dream*, including a duet of the title track with his wife. Two days later, Barack Obama walked into history.

Following the latter's electoral victory on

With the Obamas in Cleveland, 2008.

November 4th 2008 and his rousing speech in Chicago's Grant Park, Springsteen's song *The Rising* was played in celebration. The new president then repaid his gratitude to the artist again the following year. At the Obama Inaugural Celebration on January 18th 2009, Springsteen was the opening musical act. Never one to suffer from stage fright, he belted out *The Rising* with an all-female choir in front of more than 400,000, as well as a rendition of Woody Guthrie's *This Land Is Your Land* with Pete Seeger.

Having debuted selections from *Working on a Dream* while on the political trail at the back end of 2008, Springsteen released the disc on January 27th 2009. Recorded and mixed at Southern Tracks in Atlanta, Georgia, and with additional production taking place in New York City, Los Angeles and New Jersey, Springsteen's 24th album revealed his prolific songwriting abilities. His well of inspiration had been overflowing after the completion of *Magic*, with the result that he had continued to pen material while touring the latter album. Springsteen explains: "When my friend, producer Brendan O'Brien, heard the new songs, he said: 'Let's keep going!'

Campaigning for Obama, Cleveland 2008.

The 2009 Super Bowl half-time show featured the songs *Tenth Avenue Freeze-Out, Born To Run, Working On A Dream and Glory Days.*

"Over the course of the next year, that's just what we did, recording with The E Street Band during the breaks on last year's tour. I hope *Working on a Dream* has caught the energy of the band fresh off the road from some of the most exciting shows we've ever done. All the songs were written quickly, we usually used one of our first few takes, and we all had a blast making this one from beginning to end." The record-buying public responded in numbers to *Working on a Dream*, Springsteen's 16th studio creation and the last album that featured contributions from Danny Federici (as well as work by the organist's son, Jason). It went to No. 1 instantly – Springsteen's 9th album to top the charts over a period of 3 decades – and achieved gold status. Boasting a classic pop sound, *Working on a Dream* won The Boss a Grammy for Solo Rock Vocal, and its 12th track, *The Last Carnival*, paid worthy tribute to the late Federici.

"All the songs were written quickly, we usually used one of our first few takes"

True to form, Springsteen geared up for another dose of concerts to support the album, but before The Working on a Dream Tour hit the road in April, there was the minor matter of Super Bowl XLIII to attend to. On February 1st 2009, Bruce and The E Street Band provided the half-time entertainment during American football's annual jamboree. Having agreed to perform after many previous offers, Springsteen weathered a storm of promotional activity and personal appearance before the big event. For a man in his 60th year, the singer's stamina was phenomenal. Springsteen soldiered on gamely, but he did at least concede: "This has probably been the busiest month of my life."

Lasting nearly eight months,
the 84-show circus featured minimal
offerings from the new album,
concentrating instead on classics

The Working On A Dream Tour, 2009, with Max's son Jay Weinberg on drums.

Two months to the day after the Super Bowl glitz, Springsteen embarked on The Working on a Dream Tour with The E Street Band. Lasting nearly eight months, the 84-show circus featured minimal offerings from the new album, concentrating instead on classics and selections that reflected the late-2000s recession. Several gigs on the tour treated fans to entire-album performances of *Born to Run*, *Darkness on the Edge of Town*, or even *Born in the U.S.A.* Additionally, the concerts witnessed Springsteen playing songs requested by audience members holding up signs, as on the last stages of The Magic Tour.

In career terms, The Working on a Dream Tour was less lengthy than some of Springsteen's former escapades, although it still took $156 million at the box office. But the road show did constitute the first real foray into the world of music festivals for Bruce and his team: they topped the bill at the Pinkpop Festival in the Netherlands, Le Festival des Vieilles Charrues in France, the Bonnaroo Music Festival in the United States and the Glastonbury Festival and Hard Rock Calling in the UK.

In particular, the two latter gigs featured blistering sets, and Springsteen's England highlight appeared the following year on DVD as *London Calling: Live in Hyde Park* (recorded on June 28th 2009 and released on June 22nd 2010). Among their other glorious moments on the road, Springsteen and the band performed a 5-concert stint at Giants Stadium in New Jersey near the end of proceedings, with The Boss's most recent tour (to date) finishing in Buffalo, New York on November 22nd 2009. Speculation was rife that this concert marked the last performance by The E Street Band, but Springsteen stated that it was goodbye "for a little while."

The singer/songwriter's annus mirabilis also included a plethora of tribute- and benefit-concert appearances: The Clearwater Concert, a celebration of singer Pete Seeger's 90th birthday; the Rock and Roll Hall of Fame's 25th anniversary benefit concert, and a benefit for the charity Autism Speaks at Carnegie Hall. In December 2009, the 60-year-old Springsteen was ranked fourth among the top touring acts of the first decade of the 21st century by *Rolling Stone* magazine – below only The Rolling Stones, U2 and Madonna.

Hard Rock Calling, Hyde Park, London 2009.

"While I am the President, he is The Boss!"

That month he was also among the recipients of the Kennedy Center Honors (an annual award made to figures from the performing arts world for their contribution to American culture and exemplary lifetime achievement). One of 5 honourees on the occasion, Springsteen rubbed shoulders with jazz ace Dave Brubeck and also film royalty Messrs Mel Brooks and Robert De Niro.

President Obama delivered a speech in which he talked about how the singer had incorporated the life of regular Americans into his expansive palette of songs, and how his concerts surpassed the typical rock 'n' roll experience. Also how, as well as being high-octane affairs, they were "communions". Obama concluded: "While I am the President, he is The Boss!" Fair point.

As for more recent times, the last two years have evidenced Springsteen's humanitarian side and unquestionable work ethic. On January 22nd 2010 he performed with other high-profile artists on Hope for Haiti Now: A Global Benefit for Earthquake Relief – organised by the actor George Clooney to raise funds for the disaster – while in 2011 he concentrated on songwriting.

In June that year, the death of E Street Band saxophonist Clarence Clemons shifted Springsteen's focus. It was a huge loss: "Clarence lived a wonderful life... He carried within him a love of people that made them love him. He created a wondrous and extended family. He loved the saxophone, loved our fans and gave everything he had every night he stepped on stage." For the Springsteen devotee, the absence of Clemons from the 2012 Wrecking Ball Tour is a sadness, to be sure, but the accompanying album has preserved 'The Big Man' for posterity, with his sax solos featuring on 2 of the tracks.

Bruce with his fellow honorees at the Kennedy Center, 2009.

Wrecking Ball, Springsteen's 17th studio album, was released in March 2012. Its first single, *We Take Care of Our Own*, was released on January 19th, and in February, Bruce and the touring line-up of The E Street Band opened with the song at the Grammy Awards in Los Angeles. Containing 11 new tracks of the singer's material, *Wrecking Ball* is also available as a special edition that includes two bonus tracks plus exclusive artwork and photography. Springsteen's current manager Jon Landau reckons that his artiste is bang on the money with this release: "Bruce has dug down as deep as he can to come up with this vision of modern life. The lyrics tell a story you can't hear anywhere else and the music is his most innovative in recent years. The writing is some of the best of his career and both veteran fans and those who are new to Bruce will find much to love on *Wrecking Ball*."

In support of the new album, Springsteen and The E Street Band are hitting the road throughout Europe and North America this year. Covering the U.S.A. from Atlanta to Los Angeles, New York and, of course, New Jersey, the tour's European dates include Seville, Germany, Italy and the U.K. After delighting the Irish and Swedish faithful, the touring curtain will descend for good in Helsinki, although a second leg in North America is rumoured to be on the cards for late in the year. But whatever the final resting place of The Wrecking Ball Tour, one thing remains certain: The Boss is back in town!

The last concert to be held at New Jersey's Giants Stadium before its demolition, 2009. Could Bruce have found some inspiration for a new album title, perhaps?

Bring on your

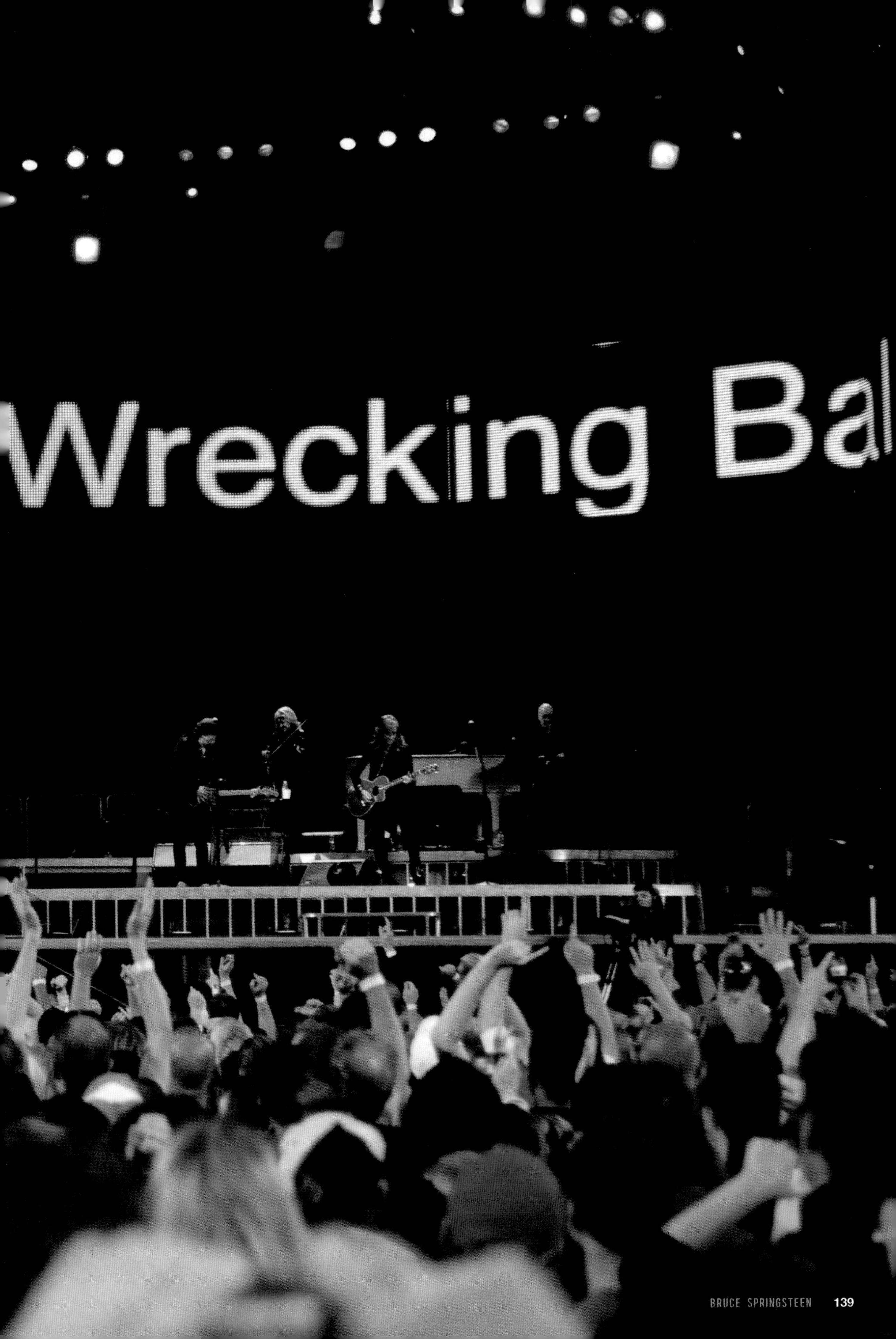
Wrecking Bal

Wearing his country influences on tour, Toronto 2009.

Elements of Latin-American music, as well as jazz, soul and funk influences could be heard.

STYLE AND SUBSTANCE

SPRINGSTEEN IS FAMED for his prolific output as a singer/songwriter. His fire of creativity never seems to be extinguished, and is sparked by various genres.

For inspiration, Springsteen has tapped into the great American traditions of popular music, blues and country. Rock 'n'

roll was a major first influence, while both his debut album, *Greetings from Asbury Park, N.J.* and the song *This Hard Land* paid tribute to the folk styles of Dylan and Woody Guthrie.

Springsteen expanded the range of his compositions with his second album, *The*

Wild, the Innocent & the E Street Shuffle. Elements of Latin-American music, as well as jazz, soul and funk influences could be heard, and the song *New York City Serenade* was reminiscent of the music of George Gershwin. Instrumentally, piano played a key role on this record and on *Born to Run*.

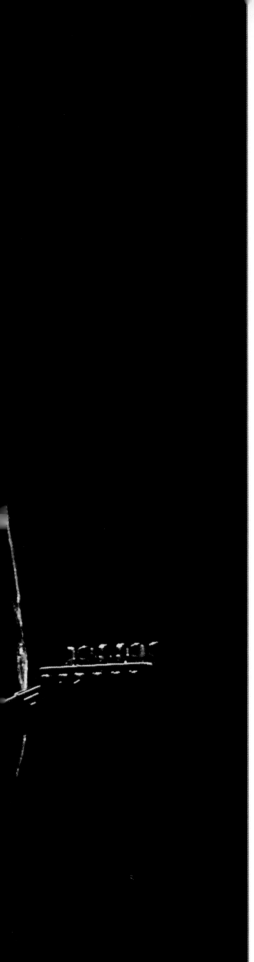

The Seeger Sessions, Asbury Park 2006.

While Springsteen had focused on the rock elements of his work early on in his career, he would compress this sound later, developing *Darkness on the Edge of Town* into a concise musical format that contained simple riffs and clearly recognisable, dominant song structures. The *Darkness* development continued on Springsteen's album *Born in the U.S.A.*, the title song of which had a constantly repeating, fanfare-like keyboard cry and a pounding drum beat. These sounds fitted Springsteen's voice, which treated listeners to the unsentimental story of a disenchanted angry figure.

In recent years, Springsteen has diversified his music once again: there are more elements of folk and gospel in the mix, while on his last solo album, *Devils & Dust*, the singer drew rave reviews for the intimate nature of his writing and his understated vocals. 2006's *We Shall Overcome: The Seeger Sessions* also marked a shift away from Springsteen's better-known brand of (poppy) rock, with its folk-band numbers and exuberant approach. All kinds of American music snuggled up together on that album – ragtime, Dixieland, gospel and French Quarter – while the subsequent tour featured folk versions of Springsteen rock songs. *Magic*, though, in 2007, created a different vibe: its energy and lush arrangements made for a great stadium-rock experience.

At the Rainforest Fund's 21st anniversary concert in 2010 with, from left, Sting, Debbie Harry, Lady Gaga, Elton John and Shirley Bassey.

As for the words that complement the music, Springsteen's lyrics have often been described as cinematic in scope: frequently they cover highly personal issues such as individual commitment, dissatisfaction and dismay with life in the context of real situations. For example, his 1978 album *Darkness on the Edge of Town* focused on the emotional struggles of working-class life.

Thematically, Springsteen has often addressed political and global concerns in his music; tunes such as this reflect his response to the events around him. A number of these songs contributed to Springsteen's stardom, while many of them cannot be clear without understanding Springsteen's political bias.

What follows is a chronological list of the political and activist causes for which the singer has campaigned publicly:

September 19th-23rd 1979: Springsteen and The E Street Band joined the Musicians United for Safe Energy anti-nuclear power collective at Madison Square Garden.

August 20th 1981: Springsteen played A Night For The Vietnam Veterans – an appeal on behalf of the Vietnam Veterans of America Foundation to "heal the physical and psychological wounds inflicted on the soldiers who fought the nation's most unpopular war."

1984: Refused several million dollars from the Chrysler Corporation to use the song *Born in the U.S.A.* in a commercial.

1985: Featured on the *We Are the World* album and song.

1988: Headlined the worldwide Human Rights Now! Tour for Amnesty International.

2004: *No Surrender* became the main campaign theme song during John Kerry's unsuccessful bid for the presidency; in the last days on the trail, Springsteen performed acoustic versions of the tune at Kerry rallies.

April 2008: Springsteen announced his endorsement of Senator Barack Obama's presidential campaign. Throughout the year, he showed his support through attendance and performance at rallies.

2009: Contributed to the soundtrack of documentary film *The People Speak* by playing guitar and harmonica.

January 2009: Opening musical act for the Obama Inaugural Celebration.

May 3rd 2009: Appeared at The Clearwater Concert.

October 29th -30th 2009: Made an

Springsteen has often addressed political and global concerns in his music.

The Harley Davidson 105th anniversary concert, Milwaukee 2008.

appearance at the Rock and Roll Hall of Fame's 25th anniversary benefit concert.

January 22nd 2010: Appeared at Hope for Haiti Now: A Global Benefit for Earthquake Relief.

Additionally, Springsteen has been associated with various local food banks for years, particularly in his native New Jersey. During concerts, he usually breaks the routine to announce his support and later matches the collection from the concert with his own money. During his Charlotte, North Carolina concert on November 3rd 2009, he began a collection for the local food bank with a personal donation of $10,000 and then matched the total take later on. He has also given substantially to workers' unions in America and Europe.

The E Street Band on stage at Madison Square Garden, New York, 2007.

MEET TH

IN THE LATE 1960s and early 1970s, Springsteen was a major player in the vibrant music scene in and around the City of Asbury Park on the Jersey Shore. As the prominent musicians of the period honed their skills in the company of Springsteen or other bands, the cream of the crop emerged as follows: saxophonist Clarence Clemons, accordion-cum-keyboard player Danny Federici, drummer Vini Lopez, pianist-cum-keyboard player David Sancious, bassist Garry Tallent and guitarist Steve Van Zandt. And when

Springsteen secured his recording contract with CBS Records in 1972, he selected the core members of the above bunch to record and then tour in support of his debut album. Founded in October 1972 and officially called The E Street Band in September 1974, this collective of musicians has been Springsteen's primary backing group (in name) ever since, even though the line-up of personnel may have changed. The singer has put together other backing bands during his career, but The E Street Band has been together more or

On stage with the band during the Human Rights Now! Tour, 1988...

Steve Van Zandt starred as Silvio Dante in the television series *The Sopranos.*

E BAND

less continuously for the past four decades. In its various guises, the band has also recorded (both individually and as a band) with a wide range of other artists including Bob Dylan, David Bowie and Lady Gaga.

When not working with Springsteen, members of the band have recorded as soloists and have pursued successful careers as session musicians, record producers, songwriters, actors, and other roles in entertainment. The most well known in their separate careers are

Max Weinberg, who has led his own band, first on *Late Night with Conan O'Brien* and then on *The Tonight Show with Conan O'Brien*, from 1993-2010, and Steve Van Zandt, who starred as Silvio Dante in the television series *The Sopranos* from 1999 to 2007.

Like any great 'squad', The E Street Band team sheet needed tweaking in its infancy. David Sancious didn't appear regularly on stage until June 1973, and Vini Lopez was asked to resign in February 1974, before being replaced by Ernest 'Boom' Carter.

...and 15 years later, still going strong in London, 2003.

A few months later, in August 1974, Sancious and Carter left to form their own jazz-fusion band called Tone. Their places were taken in September 1974 by Roy Bittan (keyboards) and Max Weinberg (drums), while Steve Van Zandt officially joined in July 1975. This line-up remained stable until the early 1980s when Van Zandt left to pursue his own career, a move that was announced in 1984 (he would rejoin in 1995). In June 1984 Nils Lofgren (guitar, vocals) was added to replace Van Zandt; Springsteen's future wife, Patti Scialfa (vocals, later guitar), also joined the team. By 2002, the group would include Soozie Tyrell on violin and vocals.

The E Street Band established its reputation among studio musicians in the 1970s and 1980s with its significant contribution to the Springsteen albums *Born to Run*, *Darkness on the Edge of Town*, *The River* and *Born in the U.S.A.* However, unlike The Silver Bullet Band or The Heartbreakers, The E Street Band never received a full credit on a Springsteen studio album: only individual members were credited. Even though the band did all or nearly all of the playing on these albums, each was released in Bruce Springsteen's name. Indeed, The E Street Band is not even mentioned as such in any of the literature for these albums until an inside liner note for *The River*, and then a cover 'Performed by' credit on *Born in the U.S.A.* Later albums such as *Tunnel of Love* and *Greatest Hits* did name the band and list the members.

Concerts were a different story. Live performances were almost always billed as Bruce Springsteen & The E Street Band, and Springsteen pointed the spotlight on the brand of the band onstage. In each concert, he typically would extend one song (between 1974 and 1984, almost always *Rosalita*) to involve an elaborate introduction of each member of the band, introducing nicknames, characterising each player ('Professor' Roy Bittan, 'Miami' Steve Van Zandt, 'Phantom' Dan Federici, 'Mighty' Max Weinberg, and Garry 'W' Tallent), whipping the audience up into a total frenzy before the final, over-the-top introduction of 'The Big Man', Clarence Clemons. More substantially, Springsteen split the concert revenues equally with the band, a practice almost unheard of for backing bands in the music industry.

Longtime E Street Band member Nils Lofgren, pictured backstage in 2006.

Springsteen's future wife, Patti Scialfa, joined the team in 1984.

With future wife Patti Scialfa, Giants Stadium 1985.

In 1989 Springsteen informed the E Street Band members that he would not be using their services for the foreseeable future. He had already recorded one completely solo album, *Nebraska*, while the last full-band activity had been autumn 1988's Human Rights Now! Tour. Band members started to go their separate ways and onto separate projects: Tallent to Nashville to work on record production, Federici to California, Clemons to Florida, Lofgren to Maryland to resume his long-time solo activities. Weinberg, apart from an abortive attempt at law school, was putting together the band Killer Joe and recording an album. In 1993 he became the bandleader on the American talk show *Late Night with Conan O'Brien* – remaining as such for its entire run. When O'Brien moved to *The Tonight Show* in 2009, Weinberg reprised his band-leading role, and the show's house band – formerly known as the Max Weinberg 7 – was redubbed Max Weinberg and the Tonight Show Band.

Despite the split in 1989, Springsteen continued to use assorted members of The E Street Band on his projects. Roy Bittan was retained for both *Human Touch* and *Lucky Town* (1992). The former included a guest appearance from David Sancious, while the latter introduced Soozie Tyrell. Patti Scialfa also provided backing vocals on both. However, the majority of musicians used on these albums were session musicians. The E Street Band was not used on the subsequent Springsteen tour either, although Bittan was called up once again and Scialfa occasionally added backing vocals; as a result of this, both featured on *In Concert/MTV Plugged*. *The Ghost of Tom Joad* saw Danny Federici, Garry Tallent, Tyrell, and Scialfa provide backing on some tracks while Federici, Tyrell and Scialfa are all present on *Devils & Dust*, even if the latter album was mainly a solo recording by Springsteen. And although individual members of the band played on *Human Touch*, *Lucky Town*, *In Concert/MTV Plugged*, *The Ghost of Tom Joad*, and *Devils & Dust*, none of these albums are regarded as E Street Band albums. *Tunnel of Love*, on the other hand, falls into a grey area and its status is open to debate.

Band members started to go their separate ways and onto separate projects.

Drummer Max Weinberg, Philadelphia 2009.

Garry Tallent (left) and Max Weinberg at the Rock 'n' Roll Hall Of Fame, 2009.

In 1995, Springsteen released the eighteen-song compendium *Greatest Hits*, for which The E Street Band was temporarily reunited to record 4 numbers. Three years later, the singer/songwriter released *Tracks*, a box-set collection of unreleased recordings dating as far back as 1972, many of which featured the band. And in 1999, The E Street Band reunited with Springsteen for real, ten years after he had dismissed them. They staged an extremely successful Reunion Tour after this, culminating in an HBO special and the album *Live in New York City* (released on March 27th 2001). With the exception of TV stars Weinberg and Van Zandt, the band members had not found any career paths that could match The E Street Band for fame and fortune. However, there appeared to be no long-term animosity after this decade of separation.

In 1999, The E Street Band reunited with Springsteen for real.

Actor and guitarist Steve Van Zandt, pictured in early 2012.

Playing with The Sessions Band, New Orleans 2006.

A year later in 2002, the reunion continued with the release of Springsteen's new studio offering *The Rising* and the lengthy, successful Rising Tour that accompanied the album. Other high-profile tours that then ensued in support of Springsteen/E Street Band albums such as *Magic* (2007) and *Working on a Dream* (2009) showed that The Boss and his cohorts were back together again more permanently. Also from this era of creative collaboration came *The Essential Bruce Springsteen* (2003), a package of greatest hits and more archive material, while The

Vote for Change tour in October 2004 marked a temporary breather for Springsteen and The E Street Band. The singer then recorded and toured his 2006 folk-rock material, *We Shall Overcome: The Seeger Sessions*, with a different group of backing musicians known as The Sessions Band. Even though E Street Band stalwarts Soozie Tyrell and Patti Scialfa appeared in The Sessions Band, Springsteen remained unclear at the time whether he would avail himself of The E Street Band's services again.

but the group's re-emergence on The Magic Tour at the end of 2007 proved the importance of its long-term association with Springsteen. Without each other, the duo was incomplete, particularly when it came to performing live.

Springsteen had always given elaborate band introductions during concerts, often incorporating humorous characterisations of band members or stories about them, and the singer's build-up to his over-the-top intro of 'Master of the Universe' Clarence Clemons was a key part of the brand. Springsteen's co-existence with his regular musicians – whether in the studio or on stage – was vital. Think America without hot dogs and you get the picture. Examples of the synchronicity between front man and his support occurred during The Reunion Tour on *Tenth Avenue Freeze-Out*, where Springsteen would pay tribute to The E Street Band's quality. The practice continued with *Mary's Place* on The Rising Tour and at the end of the Magic Tour concerts during *American Land*. On the latter road show, the video screens around the stage added cartoon-like graphics to illustrate the final "E! Street! Band!" salute.

Springsteen's co-existence with his regular musicians was vital.

Danny Federici (background), Clarence Clemons and Bruce, New Jersey 2007.

"Danny is one of the pillars of our sound and has played beside me as a great friend for more than 40 years"

The much missed Danny Federici, pictured in 2004.

When the first part of The Magic Tour came to a close on November 19th 2007, worrying times soon overshadowed the previous high jinks. Danny Federici took a break from touring to undergo treatment for melanoma, and his position in the line-up was covered by Sessions Band member Charles Giordano. The Boss provided vocal encouragement for his New Jersey-born buddy, who had been a feature of The E Street Band since 1973: "Danny is one of the pillars of our sound and has played beside me as a great friend for more than 40 years. We all eagerly await his healthy and speedy return." It was not to be a happy outcome, however. Federici did make a return to the stage on March 20th the following year for portions of a performance with Bruce Springsteen and The E Street Band in Indianapolis, but he died on April 17th 2008 at the young age of 58.

Having started the accordion at 7, The E Street Band's accomplished organist and backing vocalist had been inspired by music (and an inspiration to others) for most of his life. With characteristic magnanimity, Springsteen then dedicated his forthcoming album *Working on a Dream* (2009) to his colleague. Following the latter's death, The Danny Federici Melanoma Fund was founded in New York to treat the disease through clinical trials at the Memorial Sloan-Kettering Cancer Center. The project also aimed to raise awareness of melanoma.

A year on from the sadness surrounding Federici's illness, Springsteen and The E Street Band were the star attraction of the Super Bowl XLIII Halftime Show in Tampa, Florida on February 1st 2009. Days before the game, The Boss gave a rare press conference, during which he promised to deliver a "twelve minute party." When asked if he was nervous about performing in front of such a massive

IN THIS TEMPLE
AS IN THE HEARTS OF TH
FOR WHOM HE SAVED TI
THE MEMORY OF ABRAHAM
IS ENSHRINED FOR

audience, Springsteen alluded to his recent January 18th 2009 appearance at the "We Are One" concert at the Lincoln Memorial (pictured), a celebration of Barack Obama's Presidential inauguration: "You'll have a lot of crazy football fans, but you won't have Lincoln staring over your shoulder. That takes some of the pressure off." The Super Bowl performance by Springsteen and The E Street Band coincided perfectly with the January release of his new album *Working on a Dream*. The band's set, which went a little over the allotted 12-minute running time, included the title track as well as a cluster of reliable old favourites like *Tenth Avenue Freeze-Out*, *Born to Run* and *Glory Days*. Complementing Bruce and the team onstage were The Miami Horns and a large choir, the Joyce Garrett Singers. Two months after the Super Bowl razzmatazz, The Working on a Dream Tour took to the road. During the dates between April and November, 19-year-old Jay Weinberg followed in his father Max's footsteps by filling in occasionally on drums.

Performing The Rising at the Lincoln Memorial, 2009.

With his friend Clarence, Wembley Stadium 1985.

"We will continue to make music and perform. Let's face it, that's all we really know how to do. But it will be very different without him"

In more recent times, The E Street Band had to come to terms with another monumental loss when Clarence Clemons suffered a stroke and died from resulting complications at the age of 69 on June 18th 2011. Steve Van Zandt commented poignantly about his charismatic band mate: "We will continue to make music and perform. Let's face it, that's all we really know how to do. But it will be very different without him." Famed for his repertoire on tenor, baritone and soprano saxophones (while also providing percussion and backing vocals for The E Street Band), Clarence Clemons remains one of the most flamboyant entertainers ever to grace a stage. His musical gift was inspired by hearing gospel as a child – his grandfather was a Southern Baptist preacher – and by the time of his emergence on the Jersey Shore scene at the end of the 60s, Clemons was determined to encounter a man called Springsteen.

His recollection of their first meeting, apparently in September 1971, is the stuff of legend. Robin Hood and Little John, step aside: "One night we were playing in Asbury Park. I'd heard The Bruce Springsteen Band was nearby at a club called The Student Prince and on a break between sets I walked over there. On stage, Bruce used to tell different versions of this story but I'm a Baptist, remember, so this is the truth. A rainy, windy night it was, and when I opened the door the whole thing flew off its hinges and blew away down the street. The band were on stage, but staring at me framed in the doorway. And maybe that did make Bruce a little nervous because I just said: 'I want to play with your band,' and he said: 'Sure, you do anything you want.' The first song we did was an early version of *Spirit in the Night*. Bruce and I looked at each other and didn't say anything; we just knew. We knew we were the missing links in each other's lives. He was what I'd been searching for. In one way he was just a scrawny little kid. But he was a visionary. He wanted to follow his dream. So from then on I was part of history." Who could dispute The Big Man's verdict?

On stage in LA with Clarence, 1985.

The cast list may have changed, but the production stays the same.

The Stone Pony Club remembers a New Jersey legend, 2011.

Although arguably the most identifiable member of The E Street Band – and a tower of a man in both musical and physical terms – Clemons' departure to the great gig in the sky has not derailed the group. The cast list may have changed, but the production stays the same. In November 2011, Springsteen announced on his official website that he and The E Street Band plan to tour the US and Europe in 2012. They will play four shows in England during the summer: June 21 in Sunderland; June 22, Manchester; June 24, Isle of Wight Festival; and July 14, Hard Rock Calling in London. Other European shows will run from May to July. He also stated that the band is "excited" about the forthcoming

year, and that its new music "is almost done, but still untitled."

In January 2012, *The Hollywood Reporter* passed comment on the sound of Springsteen's latest album with The E Street Band. According to the article, *Wrecking Ball* features Bruce at his angriest yet, while its musical content is a varied mix of influences and rhythm, from hip-hop to electronic percussion and Irish folk. Produced by Ron Aniello in conjunction with Springsteen and executive producer Jon Landau, *Wrecking Ball* came out on March 6th 2012. Prior to the album's release, Springsteen announced that Jake Clemons, the nephew of Clarence Clemons, would join The E Street Band as the group's new saxophonist, sharing duties with

Clarence's nephew Jake on stage in New York, 2011.

Eddie Manion. Additional musicians will complete the line-up for The Wrecking Ball Tour: singers Curtis King and Cindy Mizelle, trombonist Clark Gayton and trumpeter Curt Ramm, all of whom have toured with Springsteen before, along with newcomer Barry Danielian on trumpet. And as for the venerable old timers of The E Street Band (listed below), it must be a case of 'here we go again'. But if it ain't broke, why bother to fix it?

Take a bow:

Bruce Springsteen: lead vocals, lead and rhythm guitar, harmonica, piano.

Patti Scialfa: backing and duet vocals, acoustic guitar, percussion.

Garry Tallent: bass guitar, tuba.

Roy Bittan: piano, keyboards.

Max Weinberg: drums, percussion.

Steve Van Zandt: lead and rhythm guitar, backing vocals, mandolin.

Nils Lofgren: lead and rhythm guitar,

pedal steel guitar, backing vocals.

(Take a bow, too):

Soozie Tyrell: violin, acoustic guitar, percussion, backing vocals.

Charles Giordano: organ, accordion, glockenspiel.

Finally, if you are fortunate enough to have tickets for the 2012 tour, may I offer some words of advice from Hollywood legend Bette Davis: "Fasten your seatbelts. It's going to be a bumpy night!"

SUGGESTED FURTHER LISTENING, READING AND VIEWING

Listening

Who's Next (1971) The Who

The Slider (1972) T. Rex

Blood on the Tracks (1975) Bob Dylan

Parallel Lines (1978) Blondie

The Great Rock 'n' Roll Swindle (1979) The Sex Pistols

Scary Monsters (and Super Creeps) (1980) David Bowie

Uprising (1980) Bob Marley & The Wailers

Flesh and Blood (1980) Roxy Music

Faith (1981) The Cure

The Unforgettable Fire (1984) U2.

Reading

The New Biographical Dictionary of Film David Thomson – 2002 – Little Brown

1001 Albums You Must Hear Before You Die General Editor Robert Dimery – 2011 – Quintessence Editions Ltd

Rock Connections: the Complete Road Map of Rock 'n' Roll Bruno MacDonald – 2010 – Omnibus Press

Taxi Driver Paul Schrader – 1990 – Faber and Faber Limited

Time Out Film Guide 2011 Edited by John Pym – 2010 – Time Out Group Ltd.

Viewing (Movies)

The Prisoner of Zenda (1952) Directed by Richard Thorpe Starring Stewart Granger, Deborah Kerr and Jane Greer

The Night of the Hunter (1955) Directed by Charles Laughton Starring Robert Mitchum, Shelley Winters and Lillian Gish

Legend of the Lost (1957) Directed by Henry Hathaway Starring John Wayne, Sophia Loren and Rossano Brazzi

Dog Day Afternoon (1975) Directed by Sidney Lumet Starring Al Pacino, John Cazal and Charles Durning

American Gigolo (1980) Directed by Paul Schrader Starring Richard Gere, Lauren Hutton and Hector Elizondo

Bachelor Party (1984) Directed by Neal Israel Starring Tom Hanks, Adrian Zmed and Tawny Kitaen

Body Double (1984) Directed by Brian De Palma Starring Craig Wasson, Melanie Griffith and Gregg Henry

Sleepaway Camp II: Unhappy Campers (1988) Directed by Michael A Simpson Starring Pamela Springsteen, Renée Estevez and Tony Higgins

Devil in a Blue Dress (1995) Directed by Carl Franklin Starring Denzel Washington, Tom Sizemore and Jennifer Beals

Vanilla Sky (2001) Directed by Cameron Crowe Starring Tom Cruise, Penélope Cruz and Kurt Russell.

Viewing (Web)

http://www.davidbowie.com/

http://www.bobdylan.com/

http://www.goentertain.tv/

http://www.radiotimes.com/film

http://brucespringsteen.net/